Angie Bowie

The Pocket Essential

BISEXUALITY

W0007538

www.pocketessentials.com

First published in Great Britain 2002 by Pocket Essentials, 18 Coleswood Road,
Harpenden, Herts, AL5 1EQ

Distributed in the USA by Trafalgar Square Publishing, PO Box 257, Howe Hill
Road, North Pomfret, Vermont 05053

A CIP catalogue record for this book is available from the British Library.

ISBN 1-903047-91-9

2 4 6 8 10 9 7 5 3 1

Book typeset by Wordsmith Solutions Ltd
Printed and bound by Cox & Wyman

Acknowledgements

The Internet, Aphrodite, Mark Bego, Paul Duncan, Michael Gassett, DZH Jones, Stacia Lipka, Dick Richards and April Sandmeyer.

CONTENTS

CONTENTS

1. Introduction

Definition

Bisexuality is the ability to be attracted to both sexes. It is a state of mind rather than body. Bisexuals include working men and women of all professions: soldiers and emperors; writers and philosophers; singers, actors and performers. Research carried out at the Harvard school of public health in 1994 found that 20.8% of men and 17.8% of women admitted to sexual relations with members of the same sex at some time in their lives.

Access to information has changed the landscape of isolation and alienation felt by teenagers of the 1950s, 1960s and 1970s. Now there are books, films, television, songs and plays that address all forms of sexuality. For those finding their feet before the 1980s, there was restrained tolerance for those whose sexual activities were not solely for procreating. There was very little acceptance or support.

> "Bisexuality is not disguised homosexuality nor is it disguised heterosexuality. It is another way of sexual expression. It is a way of being."
>
> - Dr Fritz Klein, *The Bisexual Option*

The Two-Spirited persona comes to us from the American Indians. Within the American Indian tribes, a third gender was considered natural. That spirit was channelled to shamanistic practices, warrior activities, weaving, folk medicine and herbalism. An American male nurse who visited an Apache reservation reported being surprised at a proud mother who came in to visit the priest and told him, "My 16-year-old son is attracted to other men. We need to arrange for him to be initiated with the Medicine men".

The nurse was amazed there was a respected and sanctioned role for a young person drawn to the same sex, and he noted that the mother's response was different from his own mother's. Of the 250 or so Native languages still spoken in the United States, at least 168 of them have been identified as having terms for people who are not considered male or female.

Contrast this with the Christian Fundamentalist view expressed by Jerry Falwell (a televangelical preacher in the US) in this e-mail responding to the Bisexuality essay posted on www.angiebowie.com:

'I usually start with *Genesis* 2 and *Romans* 1.You can find basic answers to this question (GAY - LESBIAN) at www.campuslife.net under 'Love and Dating' or 'Love, Sex & Real Life.' I would start with *Genesis* 1 & 2. God created Adam and Eve, not Adam and Steve. Even Jesus quoted from *Genesis* 1 & 2 when asked about marriage and divorce. For more information on this, I would recommend Ken's video *Raising Godly Children In An Ungodly World*. This will show the Biblical purpose of marriage, which is to be fruitful and multiply and to raise Godly children, neither of which can be done in a homosexual environment. You may look up the following passages in *The Bible* that speak of sexual immorality. The one from *Leviticus* is the one that directly pertains with homosexuality. *Leviticus* 18:22. *1 Kings* 14:24. *Galatians* 16-21. *Ephesians* 5:1-17. *Colossians* 3:1-6. *1 Thessalonians* 4:3- 8. Falwell: *Love The Sinner, Hate The Sin*. On Tuesday, I [Rev Jerry Falwell] met with Mel White, the nation's most recognised homosexual clergy member. Mel and I have been friends for a long time. He edited my book *If I Should Die Before I Wake*, an account of my pro-life efforts, in 1984. He has also penned books for Dr Billy Graham, Pat Robertson and Oliver North. I did not learn until 1991, when he openly disclosed his homosexuality, that Mel had embraced this lifestyle. He and his partner, Gary Nixon, have started Soulforce, Inc., a religious group supporting gay rights, in Laguna Beach, California. The occasion of our meeting this week was because Mel believes that my moral crusade for America could be perceived by a lunatic fringe to be an endorsement of hostility toward homosexuals. I have never advocated violence against any individual or group, nor would I ever do so. And, in this meeting, I agreed that my staff and I will be vigilant in assuring that we do not make any statements that can be construed as sanctioning antagonism against homosexuals. However, I want to assure my readers that I did not, in any way, alter my steadfast commitment to preaching that homosexuality is Biblically wrong. The message of God's Word is clear. Any sexual activity outside the hero sexual bonds of marriage is sin. *I Corinthians* 7:2 tells us, 'Nevertheless, to avoid fornication, let

8

every man have his own wife and let every woman have her own husband.' No matter how carefully you attempt to read between the lines of that verse, there is no suggestion of a man taking a husband or a woman taking a wife. I believe that God has given us unmistakable Divine instructions for living... and homosexuality is not a part of it. *Romans* chapter 1 reveals to us an earlier time in history when mankind manipulated Scripture in order to worship self over the Creator. 'For this cause God gave them up unto vile affections: for even their women did change the natural use into that which is against nature: And likewise also the men, leaving the natural use of the woman, burned in their lust one toward another; men with men working that which is unseemly, and receiving in themselves that recompense of their error which was met.' (*Romans* 1:26, 27) These verses require that Christians never alter or corrupt the Biblical mandate that homosexuality is sin. At the same time, God has called me to be a minister to my fellow man. I cannot do that from a perspective of condemnation. And it would be wrong for me to write off Mel White and others who have embraced this lifestyle because there is hope for change. Michael Johnston, a former homosexual who is now dying of AIDS-related illnesses, has travelled nationwide to show how a relationship with Christ can wholly change one's life. His life as 'a new creature in Christ' is a living testimony to the power of the Gospel. Therefore, I am committed to ensuring that my message is clear. The only hope for all of us - heterosexual or homosexual - is a life-changing relationship with Jesus Christ. And in so saying, I will be ever mindful to preach this message with a heart of love and not condemnation for Mel White and other homosexuals in our nation. I continue to love Mel and consider him a friend. He told me that he is just as concerned about the level of hate from the homosexual community aimed at me and other Christian leaders...'

This e-mail goes on for another couple of pages.

Eunuchs, Hijras, hermaphrodites and transsexuals are considered bisexuals because their spirits and bodies have experienced the consciousness of both genders. Eunuchs are men whose reproductive organs have been removed. Hijras[1] are found in India. They are eunuchs who dress as women; some may have been hermaphroditic at birth but their castration is a commonly-shared trait and many are transsexuals. Hermaphrodites are born with either both sets of genitalia or a small, physical genital manifestation. Transsexuals[2] are surgically altered and treated with hormonal drugs to achieve a sexual change from one gender to the other.

In India the Hijras are acquired or stolen by traders. Recently Shobha Nehru was elected to State public office in the city of Hissar. She was raised in an upper-caste family and taken away at the age of 14 by a gang of eunuchs to whom she had been promised. Jonathan Karp reports in *The Wall Street Journal* in 2001: 'But Ms Nehru belongs to a unique breed in India's rough-and-tumble, often corrupt political world. She is honest, hardworking, productive and a eunuch. For years after she was taken from her family by a gang of eunuchs, Ms Nehru dwelled in a subculture of sexual outcasts who rank lower in India than the untouchables. They are notorious for crashing weddings, singing raunchy songs and dancing until they are paid to leave. But after her election to the municipal council in this city in Northern India three years ago, Ms Nehru has outshone her peers at getting water, sewer lines and roads for her district, a transformed slum.'[3]

Eunuchs are established in Chinese and Egyptian cultures. The bisexuality of Chinese emperors is first chronicled in the fourth century BC: 'Several of the Han emperors were homosexual in the Greek pederastic sense: bisexual rather than strictly homosexual. In later times, the Chinese became suspicious of bisexuality. One writer of the Ming period (AD 1368-1644) was convinced that bisexual fathers frequently had hermaphrodite children. During the latter part of the third century, he said, when bisexuality was very common, there had been an unusually large number of hermaphrodites born. And hermaphrodites, as everyone knew, were unnatural monsters, capable of the blackest and most dastardly crimes.'[4]

In Egypt, in the tenth century AD, black and white eunuchs were employed in all areas of the government and military operations. White eunuchs, known as Saqaliba, had already been at the Fatimid court in Tunisia. Spain was the main source of Saqlabi eunuchs. The black and white eunuchs were teachers, guardians of the harem, diplomats, administrators and soldiers. Other Saqaliba were commanders of naval and land forces.[5]

One of the great eunuchs was the Chinese admiral/explorer Cheng Ho, who lived during the fourteenth and fifteenth centuries. Cheng Ho was a Muslim and his father had made the pilgrimage to Mecca. 'Ma Ho,' as he was known, proved to be an exceptional servant to Prince Zhu Di. He became an admiral in 1403, the first eunuch appointed to such a high military position in China, and was ordered to oversee the construction of a Treasure Fleet to explore the seas surrounding China. He was a tall, diplomatic but aggressive warrior. When a pirate captain attacked the Treasure Fleet, Cheng Ho captured him and sent him to China for punishment. Cheng Ho made 7 voyages with huge fleets and brought back ambassadors and treasure to China. The huge 60-70 vessel fleets had supplies of Chinese silk and treasure, water, horses, soldiers and diplomats. They travelled to Sri Lanka, Vietnam, Java, Malacca, India and Australia.

There are two other eunuchs whose experiences are recorded in their own words Ssu-ma Ch'ien 145-90 BC (he was the Grand historian of the Han court) and Peter Abelard (the great French logician and teacher).[6]

Meanwhile in the Americas, Wendy Susan Parker writes: 'In 1530 the Spanish explorer Cabeza de Vaca wrote in his diary of seeing 'soft' native Indian males in Florida tribes dressing and working as women. Later numerous reports by seventeenth-century Spanish Conquistadors in the south west and fifteenth-century writings by Catholic missionaries, French fur traders and British colonists in the north west confirmed the same phenomenon in other tribes. Cultural anthropologists later documented this 'third gender' status in at least 120 other North American tribes and in numerous other cultures around the world.'[7]

Queen Nzinga of Africa dressed as a man and had a harem of men dressed as women serve her at court.[20] She fought the Portuguese as they tried to conquer her kingdom of Ndongo to expand their empire.

Cross-dressing or 'gender borrowing' has been a statement of the existence of a third gender since the beginning or recorded cultures. There are many terms in African languages to describe mannish women and feminine men.

This practice occurred in Europe during the reign of Queen Christina of Sweden. Her father, Gustav II raised her as a boy. She inherited the throne at the age of six when King Gustav was killed in 1632. Her education was superb and she spoke 7 languages. Count Oxenstierna was her political tutor and advisor. She reigned from 1644 to 1654. In 1654 she abdicated and pursued her interest in philosophy, studying with Descartes, moving to Rome and converting to Catholicism.

The Greeks devised legends that dealt with just about every human mutation including hermaphrodites. In *The First Sex*, Elizabeth Gould Davis tells of cults of goddess worship, which preceded recorded history.[8] She discusses the roots of Druidism and the Celts. According to her, recent discoveries led to astonishing conclusions: 'In earliest Greek mythology the creative principle is Metis (female intelligence). She is the creator of all who, like Phoenician-Carthaginian Tanit, like Tiamiat, like Gaia, like Anat, creates the world without a male partner. Originally she was all female. By the time of Orpheus, however, she had become bisexual - a hermaphrodite, Mitis-Phanes, creator and begetter in one body.'[9]

The next revelation is: 'Asexual reproduction by females, parthenogenesis, is not only possible but it still occurs here and there in the modern world, perhaps as an atavistic survival of the once only means of reproduction in an all female world. Since the discovery of the proof of parthenogenesis by Jacques Loeb in 1911, it has been known that the male is not necessary for reproduction and that a simple physico-chemical agent in the female is enough to bring it about.'[10]

In the past bisexuals were characterised as treacherous and deceitful individuals. This assumption may have gestated the myths and legends designed to camouflage the importance of women's role in world history. Perhaps, as Davis suggests, we are the rubble of a previous civilisation which is much more advanced than our ten thousand years. That changes everything; does it not?

12

Media

The publication of *The Bisexual Option* by Dr Fritz Klein gave bisexuality a form that had dimension and character. He adapted the Kinsey scale for bisexual needs and framed his book with the research from his bisexual patients.[11]

Previously, there was no available material about sexuality and now people moan that sex is everywhere. Writers, including Michel Foucault, Gore Vidal, Fritz Klein, Susie Bright, Camille Paglia and Marjorie Garber, have contributed to people's awareness of bisexuality as a lifestyle. Michel Foucault's *History Of Sexuality* (in three volumes, English translation 1978) identifies the confessional nature of sexuality.

Being identified by one's sexual orientation is relatively new in the history of humankind, going back only to the nineteenth century. Now, however, people act as if this classification of human sexuality is a fixed axiom in relationships between people.[12]

Gore Vidal defines the sexual climate 30 years ago in *The City And The Pillar*: 'All human beings are bisexual. Conditioning, opportunity and habit account finally (and mysteriously) for sexual preference and homosexualists are quite as difficult to generalise about as heterosexualists.'

Does that matter? Is it important? Do we care?

It matters if you are in American marketing - 25-30 million people with a common denominator are not a figure to be sneezed at! It is important if we are in the throes of a sexual identity crisis and we want information. We care when it is someone we know or someone close to us, and we fear discrimination.

Do we have to decide the sex of the person we fall in love with before we meet them? Why is one sex more acceptable than another?

What is and is not acceptable often depends upon what is fashionable. The media shows trends within our society and presents role models for us to follow. Camille Paglia, an academic entertainer, coined the term Sexuals in her book *Sexual Personae*. Sexuals are characters whose work or victimisation provoke change.

Bisexuality's acceptance has been stoked by Sexuals: their writing; the model of their lives; or the results inspired by their sexual orientation. For these reasons a person's sexuality becomes more than a subject of gossip but an investigation into their motivation and how they handled situations, etc.

So, what next? In 2001 I asked Jude Rawlins (songwriter, composer and vocalist for Subterraneans) to define how he felt about sexuality as a musician and artist:

"A quote on Bisexuality? Hmm. Well, I strongly believe that love is love regardless of which way the loins twitch. And, at the end of the day, hetero, bi or gay, we can never truly be fulfilled if we give gender too much importance. A satisfactory relationship is a combination of two minds dancing, unconditional love (or as near as we can get) and a shared sense of the ridiculous. I guess bisexuality doubles your chances of finding these things.

A little oversimplified maybe. Romantic slush, even. But my journey has been far more emotional than sexual, so understanding my sexuality is part of understanding how I can love and be loved. So I find it very easy to have platonic relationships, because gender is never going to be a major reason for finding someone interesting or identifying with them.

Do you think there is such a thing as intellectual sexuality? That people may be drawn by masculine or feminine intellects, regardless of physical gender? That's just a thought. I'm not truly versed in the subject. There you see - I've learned something about myself from you already. That's the magic of communication & language.

My final thought on the subject for now: The Romans and the Greeks, even the ancient Egyptians, often blurred the so-called 'gender roles' and created some of the most celebrated homo-erotic art in history. Conventional thinking on sexuality only really seems to be as old as Christianity. I don't think that can be a coincidence. I think there is evidence to suggest that we'd evolved far beyond gender roles thousands of years ago, and that our continued sexual evolution was simply halted, along with everything else, by the arrival of religious doctrines. It may even be that defining oneself as 'heterosexual' or 'homosexual' is a relatively new idea, exactly as labelling oneself with a specific religious or political allegiance is. The pre-Christian religions had different gods - and goddesses - for everything, which at least meant there was room for personal conflict, growing pains, self-belief, etc. It wasn't until someone wrote down 'the rules'/scriptures that the concepts of differing sexualities even really emerged."

Yes, I do believe in intellectual sexuality. That's what makes me bounce out of bed every morning and attack life.

Bisexuality is a profitable keyword. In the last decade, bisexuality has emerged on cover stories in *Newsweek* and many major periodicals. Al Kielwasser's commented in *Media Watch*, 14 July 1995: '*Newsweek*'s July 17th cover story declares a new sexuality emerges... now it's coming out in the open... Of course Bisexuality is hardly a new sexuality. But it is news to much of the mainstream press and the public. It is a welcome contribution to bi-visibility.'

The New York *Time Out* has had several front-page stories on bisexuality and homosexuality including the 11-18 October 2001 'coming out' issue. My favourite coming-out story is the following, from Ellen Abrams, 47, Ad Rep: 'I have this dream of a general strike for gay, lesbian and bisexual people. Instead of coming out, we'd have one day where we'd all stay at home instead. We wouldn't go to work and we wouldn't go to school. We'd spend all day in bed or something. We'd just stay home and show the world how many of us there really are.'

The media records history. The media covers and discovers history. Then the artsy side of the media - theatre, film and music - idealises and interprets what is happening in the world to give us alternative histories. In recent years, the dominant media have been newspapers, magazines, books, radio, cinema and television.

However, within a few short years, we have witnessed the surprising development of communication technology that now gives individuals the power to communicate with the world. The Internet has played an important part in softening attitudes and allowing different folk to get to know each other without fear. People enjoy sharing mutual interests and celebrating their differences. The Internet has helped in the familiarisation of our planet's inhabitants with the customs and cultures of their local and far-flung neighbours.

'In Elizabethan England, where young boys played all the feminine roles on the stage, the device of having a boy play a romantic role of a girl disguised as a boy and fall in love with a man

15

had almost infinite possibilities of amusement for the court and the crowd alike. At other times groups of writers, artists and musicians and men and women related to the theatre have cultivated bisexuality out of a delight with personality, regardless of race, class or sex.'

- Margaret Mead, anthropologist, 1901-1978

Politics

The American writer James Baldwin (1924-1987) wrote: 'I think Americans are terrified of feeling anything. And homophobia is simply an extreme example of the American terror that's concerned with growing up. I never met a people more infantile in my life. It's a way of controlling people. Nobody really cares who goes to bed with whom finally, I mean the state doesn't really care. They care that you should be frightened of what you do. As long as you feel guilty about it, the state can rule you. it's a way of exerting control over the universe, by terrifying people.'

According to an article by Annalee Newitz and Jillian Sandell, 'Bisexuality And How To Use It: Toward A Coalitional Identity Politics,' the events of the last 30 years have destabilised the political status quo because of the mixed messages that, they claim, are being sent: 'Clearly while bisexuals can be what Fritz Klein calls sequential bisexuals, that is monogamously attached to one gender at a time, this is not the dominant understanding of bisexual habits. Even among bisexuals themselves, non-monogamy is often the 'practice' for the 'theory' of bisexuality.'

In this time after AIDS, bisexuality as a lifestyle has changed from promiscuous to sequential. Where bisexuality might have included a hot spot for two to three years during the 1970s with a couple of Bacchanalian orgies, the necessity for monogamy to promote healthy living is now the plimsoll line for satisfactory human sexual relationships.

Spirituality

"It is fairly well known that particular societies at different historical times socially approved of homosexual and bisexual liaisons. In the centuries before the Christian era, Greek art and literature assumed that virtually everyone responded at different times both to homosexual and to heterosexual stimuli.'

- Sister Jeannine Gramick c. 1986

Historically, the repression of homosexuals and bisexuals is in direct response to their association with Christians and Jewish religions. Why is this? I'm with James Baldwin on this one: fear. The Jewish doctrine had to set limits against the paganism of the ancient empires of Rome and Greece. The Rabbis controlled the legislature, so there was little division of Church and State. The Rabbis had a hand in every aspect of life. They collected taxes, prescribed Kosher food (this combated the sub-standard preservation processes then used to keep food fresh) and authorised sexual practices (women thrown out of the matrimonial bed during the time of their menses).

Next door, the customs of Islam were cruel and unusual towards women. Some members of Islam circumcised the women so that their only function was that of a brood mare as opposed to an individual with any ability to feel pleasure. They could be expelled from the husband's house after he said "I divorce you" three times.

We act surprised that there is discrimination against those who have different sexual preferences and yet millions of us were raised in one of these three perversions of religious behaviour: Judaism, Christianity and Islam. After the formation of the Christian churches, the attitude to homosexuality worsened because they took much of their discriminatory practices from the *Old Testament* and interpretations of the *Torah*.

As Robert Gordis wrote in his essay 'Homosexuality Is Not On A Par With Heterosexual Relations': 'The sexual codes in the *Torah* describe male homosexuality as an 'abomination' punishable with death like other major infractions of the moral code, such as incest and sexual contact with animals (Lev. 18:22 - 20:13)'

What a difference there is between the attitudes of Christian thinkers and the Native American Indians, as Terry Tafoya explains in his 1992 essay 'Native Gay And Lesbian Issues: The Two-Spirited': 'When Native American people discovered Columbus five centuries ago, they presented a unique conundrum of identity. Not only did most tribes not organise themselves by Kings and Queens in European Tradition, but the majority classified members as having more than two genders. This radical (for Europeans) way of seeing the world brought swift and tragic responses. The Spanish explorer Balboa, for example declared such individuals who were not considered male or female to be 'sodomites' and literally had them torn apart by his dogs in the sixteenth century. Thus from the very beginning of European contact, Native people learned not to openly discuss matters of sexuality and gender with the newcomers, because they could be killed for being 'different.''

Spirituality is a personal mission. To be at peace, you must come to terms with what you believe. If you have evolved your own set of beliefs, you are way ahead.

If, on the other hand, you are a member of a religion and want understanding and approval for your sexuality, which does not conform with their norm, you may be in for a rude awakening. If you go to church for a useful purpose, like for a country club, childcare or business/social interaction you may be better off just avoiding a conversation which includes 'coming out' to your church.

There are plenty of self-designed spiritual disciplines and plenty of other doctrines you can cleave to if you so desire. Tony Schwartz's ambitious book *What Really Matters* tackles his Pilgrim's Progress through a major sampling of physical and mental disciplines. He is indefatigable: first Ram Dass, Psychedelics and the Journey to the East, Esalen, the Yoga of the West, Betty Edwards and the Right Side of the Brain, Connecting the Mind and the Body, Flow, Learned Optimism and the Toughness Model. The man is all over the place and puts the spiritual mindset into its proper perspective.

If you are bisexual or homosexual and feel alienated by the religion in which you were raised maybe it's time to give some thought as to why you would be involved in something that is not contributing to your wellbeing.

Sister Jeannine Gramick argues eloquently about what is and isn't natural: 'Between the fifteenth and nineteenth centuries most theologians writing on sexuality divided sexual sins into two categories: those in

18

accordance with nature (i.e. open to procreation) and those contrary to nature (i.e. inhibiting procreation). Thus anal and oral intercourse, masturbation, bestiality, coitus interruptus and intercourse during pregnancy were considered unnatural: adultery, fornication and rape were considered sinful but natural.'

There is no right or wrong about human behaviour. If we become one gender and procreate by cloning, should we be denied physical interaction?

Social

Bisexuality is more than sexual preference. It is also a framework of social, emotional, behavioural and ideal preferences. We all have a need to belong but first we must accept ourselves as we are before we look for society's acceptance.

There are some societies where bisexuality is an acceptable sexuality: the Native Americans; the Chinese; the Japanese; the Tanala of Madagascar; the Largo of East Africa; the Koniag of Alaska; the Chuckchee of Siberia; the Siwans of Africa; the Keraki of New Guinea. These are hardly mainstream! In the past, the Far East also tolerated homosexuality and bisexuality. From ancient to modern times same-sex behaviour has been acceptable in China and Japan.

In China, where male brothels were common, boys were trained for prostitution by their parents. During Japan's feudal times male homosexual love was considered more manly than heterosexual love. Male geishas were prevalent until the middle of the nineteenth century and still existed until they were suppressed at the end of World War Two by the American occupation forces.

Dr Fritz Klein wrote: 'To the Kukukuku people of New Guinea, for example, such relations are an essential condition for growth into the complete man who is competent to survive as both tribal member and warrior. This practice of homosexuality is coupled with the practice and responsibility of heterosexuality, and helps keep the number of births in balance. Another example of socially sanctioned bisexuality is provided by the Batak people of Lake Toba in northern Sumatra, who have an unchanging tradition of homosexual relationships between men and boys before marriage. Once married however - and no man is permitted to remain in the single state - monogamy is the rule.'[13]

Terry Tafoya refers to the removal of Native American children from their tribes and families to be educated at boarding schools in a western manner, which dilutes the chances of Native American culture being preserved. This forced segregation has had a devastating impact on the communities as a whole. Critical teachings and attitudes regarding sexuality and gender that would have been provided at the time of puberty, for example, were never passed on in many families and tribes because the young person was away at boarding school. This practice continues to this day.

Those who disapprove of a bisexual lifestyle parrot two issues: bisexuality does not exist; and bisexuality is a neurosis. Thanks to Dr Klein, we have a list of the arguments themselves. These are the debatable polarities of bisexuality: 'A person is either gay or straight; there is no such entity as bisexuality. The bisexual is really a homosexual. Bisexuality is only a transition stage. Or the four neurotic myths of bisexuality: The bisexual is by definition neurotic; The bisexual cannot love deeply; The bisexual is mixed up and can't make up his or her mind; The bisexual is hyper-sexed and sex crazy.'[14]

By the end of the twentieth century, popular role models were profiting from the allure of the term 'Bisexual.' Bette Midler said in 1973: "What I want to be is a bisexual fantasy. I want to be the most loved, the most desired, loved woman on earth."

Madonna followed Midler, as Mark Bego wrote in *Madonna, Blind Ambition*: 'Madonna is a brilliant sexual marketer. Especially in her 1993 *SEX* book, she courted and visualised and enacted every type of fetish and fantasy that human sexuality has to offer. Her images of lesbianism, titillating male homosexuality and group sex of every gender combination made sure that she appealed to every group of sexual adventurers. She has kept us guessing for years about her own sexuality.'

Madonna constructed an elaborate relationship with fashion designers. Her choices ensured she was sat squarely on the fence of bisexuality. When Jean Paul Gaultier dressed her in caricatured female dominatrix garb, Madonna appealed to both gay and straight men and women. How-

20

ever, she was not the first to use fashion and music to communicate a message of sexual freedom.

After World War Two, the soldiers who came home were reunited with a grateful nation. However, the African American soldiers who had fought bravely were still discriminated against in the South and so the attitude of the Americans who had not fought the war was 'business as usual.' The men and women who had been posted overseas evaluated the different customs and compared them to their lives when they returned home. The government examined the politics of writers and actors, producers and musicians who proposed a policy contradictory to the commonly held American view. The House Un-American Activities Committee interrogated people who they felt had associations with their enemies. The Stalin purges in Russia had alienated the American government to the point they couldn't see straight. Out of this environment of fear and perdition came Rock 'n' Roll!

11 July 1951 was the first broadcast of Alan Freed's R&B radio show at WJW in Cleveland. By September 1952 the first edition of the TV show *American Bandstand* had been broadcast from Philadelphia. On 14 January 1954, Alan Freed had a concert in New York at the Saint Nicholas Arena called Rock 'n' Roll Jubilee. That July, Elvis Presley cut his first single, 'That's All Right Mama.'[15]

In July 1955, Bill Haley and the Comets had a number 1 song 'Rock Around The Clock.' In 1956, Hollywood joined the Rock 'n' Roll craze sweeping the country. Hollywood produced 6 films featuring rock music: *Don't Knock the Rock*; *The Girl Can't Help It*; *Rock Around the Clock*; *Shake, Rattle and Roll*; *Rock Pretty Baby*; and *Love Me Tender*. The stars of these films were diverse in their appeal: Bill Haley and His Comets; Little Richard; Alan Freed; Fats Domino; The Platters; Gene Vincent; Eddie Cochran; Big Joe Turner; Sal Mineo; and Elvis Presley. Women's roles were purely decorative in the initial stages of this new craze. And then we got Aretha Franklin in 1961 when Berry Gordy formed Motown Records in Detroit.

As fashion integrated with popular culture, the taboos surrounding what you could and couldn't do sexually were also questioned and dismantled. Young men were enticed into putting down their weaponry and

21

follow fashion. Young women started to control and determine the course of their lives.

Flamboyant sexual innovators included Liberace, whose television show introduced women to the pleasures of a soft-spoken sweet friend who soothed your nerves and made everything better, a man who was kind and sweet but demanded no sexual repartee from his behaviour. This was a turn-up for the books. There was Little Richard who preferred young men, Hugh Hefner and his Playboy clubs for the straight and faithfully challenged! The Kinsey Report made it respectable to discuss sexuality publicly.

By the 1960s, The Rolling Stones, The Beatles, Jim Morrison and The Doors, Janis Joplin ("My music isn't supposed to make you wanna riot! My music is supposed to make you wanna fuck!"), Joan Baez, Jefferson Airplane and The Beach Boys filled the airwaves with a new sensual read on the planet. And the Stones were sexually rampant: there was Mick and Marianne, Mick and Brian, Mick and Keith, Mick and Bianca, Mick and European drag queens, Mick and David, Mick and Jerry...

In the 1970s, Elton John, David Bowie, Roxy Music and Alice Cooper took the freedom of the music and sexuality and partied for a decade. Their vision was androgynous but their behaviour was myopic. Taking a sexual position and announcing it publicly to the rabid tabloid newspapers was a gold card for profile. It seemed foolish not to use the tool when it presented itself.

Debbie Harry was Punk's first sex kitten, whilst The Sex Pistols reminded everyone that pop music was supposed to be about being dissatisfied, drugs and nihilism. After many years of rampant sexuality where partying and orgies were just clean fun, the spectre of AIDS loomed over the 1980s. AIDS terminated promiscuous sexual behaviour.

Rock n' Roll is the soundtrack of our adolescence, the time when we are selecting and comparing mates deciding what we are prepared to tolerate and gambling that this major relationship will last! Our goal in relationships is intimacy; to find someone with whom we can relate. We accommodate sexual needs to find a similar heart. It is a gift to find someone who supports and comforts and brings one to climax.

We learn behaviour associated with a certain gender's function in society. If we reject society for one reason or another then we reject being told how to behave.

We follow a pilgrim's progress to achieve a full life. Living fully is a prerequisite to dying without regret. If we live fully, we die happy. If we feel like we missed out, we die wanting to stretch the time and accomplish more.

In the 1960s, living with someone without being married was considered radical, but acceptable if you were a heterosexual couple. The disapproval grew if you were a same-sex couple and very few people volunteered that information in mixed company. All sexuality was at issue: homosexuality, lesbianism, bisexuality and interracial marriages.

We see a change in the twenty-first century. Each generation clarifies the views we fought so hard to achieve. The new generation seems comfortable with their sexuality and the desire to experiment has become a preface to making choices as far as sexual identity is concerned. You could call this progress.

2. Historic Figures

'Homosexuality and bisexuality can be considered natural
because they are as old as the human race itself.'

- Goethe

In 1979, Dr Fritz Klein published *The Bisexual Option*. In the book's
foreword, Dr Regina Rheinhardt tells us that at the time of researching the
book, there were no source books about bisexuality in the New York public library. Nothing had been written save for mentions in books on homosexuality and usually as a disparagement. There was no information
connecting the lives and adventures of well-known historical characters
such as Alexander the Great, Julius Caesar and Virginia Woolf with tales
of their bisexuality. There was no context within which to apply the lessons of their lives to our own sexuality. Heroes influence us whether they
live now or their examples spring from the past. They have bequeathed
their life lessons in their actions, art or documents.

'Through the nightly loving of boys, a man, on arising, begins to
see the true nature of beauty.'

- Plato, c. 428-348 BC, Greek philosopher

In Ancient Greece, bisexuality was a part of the culture. The Hetairi
('wild' women as opposed to respectable matrons) had companions and
the Greek citizens who tutored or apprenticed youths often indulged in
sexual relationships with their young students. Such behaviour was
accepted as part of growth and learning.

Did the Greeks practice bisexuality? Yes, if we mean by this that a
Greek could simultaneously or in turn be enamoured of a boy or a girl, and
that it was common for a male to change to a preference for women after
'boy-loving' inclinations in his youth. We can talk about their bisexuality,
thinking of the free choice they allowed themselves between the two
sexes, but for them this option was not referred to as a dual, ambivalent
and bisexual structure of desire. To their way of thinking, what made it
possible to desire a man or a woman was simply the appetite that nature
had implanted in man's heart for 'beautiful' human beings whatever their
sex might be.[16]

Does this mean that the Greek women were emancipated and having a blast? 'Women played no part in Athenian high culture. They could not vote, attend the theatre or walk in the stoa talking philosophy. But the male orientation of classical Athens was inseparable from its genius. Athens became great not despite but because of its misogyny. Male homosexuality played a similar catalytic role in renaissance Florence and Elizabethan London. At such moments, male bonding enjoys an amorous intensity of self-assurance, a transient conviction of victory over mothers and nature. For 2,500 years, western culture has fed itself on the enormous achievements of homosexual hybrids, small bands of men attaining visionary heights in a few concentrated years of exaltation and defiance.'[17]

The Greeks reinforced their defiant culture with a band of gods and heroes whose sexuality was vivid and exciting. 'Aphrodite, for example, goddess of sexual intercourse, was born from the foam...According to Hesiod's *Theogony*, Cronos son of Earth and Heaven castrated his father with a billhook and hurled his testicles into the sea. They drifted away in the foam of their own semen, and it was from this that Aphrodite was born.'[18]

Homer and Hesiod recorded an observed body of behaviour. 'The heroes were as lusty as the gods. Heracles, admired by all the peoples of Greece for his strength, courage and tenacity, was said to have ravished fifty virgins in a single night'; bisexual, he also had an affair with his nephew Iolaus and fell in love with 'sweet Hylas, he of the curling locks.'[19]

Here are a few people who have shown bisexual tendencies:

Sappho (630-580 BC)

Born at Eressos on the isle of Lesbos, Sappho married a prosperous merchant and had a daughter named Cleis. Her wealth afforded her the opportunity to live her life as she chose; she spent her time studying the arts.

In the seventh century BC, Lesbos was a cultural centre. Sappho travelled widely throughout Greece. Political activities exiled her to Sicily for a time. In Sicily she became known as a poet and the residents of Syracuse erected a statue to her. Sappho composed her own music and refined the prevailing lyric meter to Sapphic meter, part of a new wave of Greek lyrists. They presented the views of the individual and not the viewpoint of the gods. She described love and loss as it affected her personally.

Her style was sensual and melodic; primarily songs of love, yearning and reflection. Most commonly the target of her affections was female, often one of the many women sent to her for education in the arts. She nurtured these women, wrote poems of love and adoration to them, and when they eventually left the island to be married, she composed their wedding songs.

While she lived, coins of Lesbos were minted with her image. Plato elevated her from the status of great lyric poet to one of the muses. Upon hearing one of her songs, Solon, an Athenian ruler, lawyer and also a poet, asked that he be taught the song "because I want to learn it and die."[21]

Socrates (469-399 BC)

Socrates studied gymnastics, music, geometry, astronomy and the doctrines of Greek thought and culture. He sculpted as a youth, but abandoned art for a divine mission to enlighten men as to their potential promoting their intellectual and moral improvement. Socrates married but his wife was difficult: 'The shrewishness of his wife Xanthippe became proverbial.'

Alcibiades was a favourite of Socrates and though half the historians make a case for their relationship never being physical, they are dreaming. 'There was for example, the occasion on which Socrates' young disciple, Alcibiades, arrived at a dinner party to find the master comfortably sharing a couch with his host. "Oh yes," said the young man crossly. "You would move heaven and earth to sit next to the best-looking person in the room!" Socrates turned to his host, "My love for that fellow is always landing me in trouble," he said. "Ever since I fell for him, I have not been allowed even to glance at a good-looking boy, far less talk to one. He gets jealous straight away...I'm afraid one of these days he'll go for me in earnest.'[22]

Alcibiades' role is important according to Camille Paglia. 'Alcibiades represents the 'the first of the beautiful boys.' This 'sexual persona' was the beginning of a character underscored throughout history from the court in Athens to the splendour of Rome, through the Crusades when the minstrel kept the faith alive; to the Renaissance and the genius of painters and sculptors and inventors: Michelangelo and Leonardo Da Vinci. The beautiful young male was deified in sculpture: the statue of David, the disciples at the last supper etc. The Elizabethans produced cross-dressing theatrical events written by playwrights like William Shakespeare who allowed the androgyny of the human spirit to fly free. This appreciation of human behaviour and motivation touched both genders in the audience.'[23]

Socrates practised minimalism: "To want nothing is divine; to want as little as possible is the nearest possible approach to the divine life." He was observant, acute and thoughtful. He developed these qualities by constant and systematic use.

In 399, Socrates was indicted as an offender against public morality. The accusation was "Socrates is guilty, firstly, of denying the gods recognised by the state and introducing new divinities, and, secondly, of corrupting the young." To the irritation of the judges and the distress of his friends, Socrates declared that for services rendered to the city, he did not deserve to be punished but rewarded as a public benefactor. The majority of judges decreed the death penalty. Socrates drank the poison.

Alexander the Great (356-323 BC)

Alexander the Great was the rock star of antiquity; he took his Hellenic crusade very seriously and defeated the Persians at Issus (Turkey) and then marched on and was accepted as Pharaoh of Egypt. An oracle had predicted that he was a son of Zeus. In 327 he was able to put a stop to the fighting in northern Iran by marrying Roxanne, one of the warring tribes' chief's daughters. Later, Alexander married Barsine-Stateira, she was Darius' daughter (King of Persia and one of Alexander's recent foes). Hephaestion married her sister.

Alexander and Hephaestion were sexually and emotionally involved throughout their lives. The boyhood friends felt like the two heroes, Achilles and Patroclus, from *The Iliad*, Alexander's favourite book. Spirituality played a part in Alexander's interaction with his various lovers and wives. 'Beginning his career simply as a member of the King's own cavalry regiment, Hephaestion's unexpected death nearly unseated Alexander's reason. For twenty-four hours Alexander lay on the body until his friends dragged him off by force; for three days he fasted, could only lie weeping, and was unapproachable. He forbade all music in court and camp, ordered

27

mourning in every city in the empire, and dedicated to Hephaestion to bear his name in perpetuity.'[24]

When he defeated Darius III of Persia, amongst the spoils of war, he was given the youngest court eunuch, a singer and dancer.

The Romans copied the Greeks. They had comparable divinities: Zeus and Jove; Aphrodite and Venus and so on. Their empire spread over most of Northern Africa, through Europe and they sought to explore further east. The Roman government built roads and guarded them to ensure the safety of trade routes, viaducts delivered water to cities; they built temples, coliseums, theatres, arenas, temples and civic buildings. They added ornamentation; everything was inspired by Greek example. Landscaping, statues and murals, portraits and ceramic, paving, mosaic and stucco work were incorporated into the physical evidence of their culture. They minted coins of gold and silver. And like the Greeks, the Romans practised bisexuality: 'The Roman annalists give us the riveting gossip. Sodomy was reported of the emperors Tiberius, Nero, Galba, Otho, Commodus, Trajan and Elagabalus. Even Julius Caesar was rumoured to be bisexual. Hadrian fell in love with the beautiful Antinous, deified him after his death and spread his image everywhere. Caligula had a taste for extravagant robes and women's clothes. He dressed his wife Caesonia in armour and paraded her before the troops. He loved impersonations and appearing in wig and costume as singer, dancer, charioteer, gladiator, virgin huntress and wife. He posed as all the male and female gods. As Jupiter he seduced many women, including his sisters.'[25]

Gaius Julius Caesar (101-44 BC)

Gaius Julius Caesar was born in 101 BC and took the title 'Dictator for Life' in 44 BC. Caesar was known to be intimate with King Nicomedes. Curio called him 'the queen's rival, the inner partner of the royal couch.'

Caesar had same-sex love affairs as well as affairs with Eunoe the Moor, wife of Bogudes, and Cleopatra, with whom he often feasted until daybreak. Cleopatra wanted to take a cruise to Ethiopia but Caesar had to decline, his troops refused to go. The elder Curio called him 'every woman's man and every man's woman.'

'Late Rome oscillated between fatigue and brutality. castration in the mother-cults was a sacrificial dependenc the empire however, the whipping got kinky, and castrates sional. Packs of them in wigs, makeup and garish female d the towns and highways clinking cymbals and begging for alms ...us describes them "squeaking for delight in their splintering harsh womanish voices." Eunuchs had a high profile in the empire. Church leaders despised them. Christian sex roles date from this period of crass, flamboyant personae.'[26]

Richard, the Lion-Heart (1157-1194)

Richard was one of three sons born to Henry II and Eleanor of Acquitaine in September 1157. Richard was lord of an empire that stretched from the Scottish border to the Pyrenees. The result of being raised at the Anjou court prompted Richard to undertake a new crusade in conjunction with Philip the king of France. Richard was partial to Philip:

'They ate every day at the same table and from the same dish, and at night their beds did not separate them. And the king of France loved him as his own soul; and they loved each other so much that the king of England [Richard's father] was absolutely astonished at the passionate love between them and marvelled at it.'[27]

Richard married Princess Berengaria (from Navarre) in Cyprus but didn't see that much of her once they were married. After attacking Saladin, the Crusaders discussed a settlement. An interview was planned between the two sides for an exchange of prisoners. The Muslims were late; so Richard executed 2,700 captives. On his way back to Europe, Leopold, Duke of Austria, captured Richard. He was thrown in a dungeon and legend has it that the troubadour Blondel heard his king singing and responded with a song that both of them knew. Whether true or not the fact remains that Eleanor, Richard's mother wrote to the Pope for assistance in the matter. Soon a ransom of 150,000 marks was set and Eleanor brought it to the Emperor in Cologne. On 2 February 1194, Richard was freed. He returned to England to set his kingdom in order but was later wounded and died when trying to collect some taxes.

Michelangelo (1475-1564)

Michelangelo Buonarotti was born in Florence to a wealthy family of bankers distantly related to the Medicis. He was commissioned by 9 Catholic popes to beautify the Italian cities. His first patron was the astonishing Lorenzo (the Magnificent) de' Medici, a renowned humanist, philosopher and patron of the arts.

Romantic biographers would like Michelangelo to have been attracted to Contessina de' Medici, the youngest daughter of Lorenzo de' Medici...They moved in different worlds. If Michelangelo sought relations with women, they came from a more humble station, where favours were dispensed more readily or were exchanged for money. Relations with men were more possible and probably more frequent. In the Medici household, Michelangelo was among a group of exceptionally learned and cultivated men with homosexual inclinations - both physically and philosophically: Angelo Poliziano, Marsilio Ficino and Lorenzo de' Medici himself. Michelangelo was probably not the initiator of relations but rather the passive recipient of their attentions - a situation extremely common in Renaissance Florence. In turn, they offered a home that was intellectually stimulating, above moral scrutiny, and without economic or mundane obligations.[28]

Michelangelo spent time working in Florence and Rome. He became a landowner in 1506. After 5 or 6 years he was a millionaire by careful investment. He purchased properties and rented them.

In Rome, Michelangelo was attracted to persons of high social station; his friendship with Tommaso dei Cavalieri continued to the artist's death, though perhaps without its initial passionate intensity. Michelangelo was friends with Vittoria Colonna, an accomplished poetess whom he met while he was working on the Last Judgement.

Michelangelo lived through the reigns of thirteen popes and worked for nine of them. For most of his long life, he lived with one or two assistants, a male servant/secretary, and a female cook and housemaid. Michelangelo never married, but this was not uncommon among Renaissance artists. Instead he formed lasting attachments with friends and was loyally committed to his family.

He outlived his friends and family. He was completely devastated, however, by the death of Urbino, his faithful servant and companion of twenty-five years. Revealing the depth of his emotions, Michelangelo wrote to his nephew of 'his intense grief, leaving me so stricken and troubled that it would have been easier to have died with him.' It is characteristic that he provided for Urbino's widow and also took an active interest in her fatherless child.

William Shakespeare (1564-1623)

William was born, baptised and buried in Stratford-upon-Avon. He was born to Mary Shakespeare née Arden and John Shakespeare. In 1582, he married Anne Hathaway - he was 18 and she was 26. In 1583 their daughter Susanna was born. Susanna was joined by the births of Hamnet and Judith who were twins. By 1592 Shakespeare was well known enough to be critiqued and included in the scathing or complimentary mentions that accompanied new works on stage.

Shakespeare's acting ensemble included Will Kempe (the leading comedian), Richard Burbage (the leading tragedian) and himself. From 1592, the Lord Chamberlain's Men and subsequently the King's Men toured, and then formed a company, which built the Globe Theatre. It was the exclusive arena for the performance of Shakespeare's plays.

'Shakespeare is an alchemist. In his treatment of sex and personality, Shakespeare is a shape-shifter and master of transformations. He returns dramatic impersonation to its ritual origins in the cult of Dionysus, where masks were magic.'[29]

He utilises cross-dressing to ferret out the information of relationships between the protagonists.

'Shakespeare's Portia is momentarily transvestite in *The Merchant Of Venice* where she wears a lawyer's robe for one act...Rosalind and Viola are sexual instigators, the cause of irksome romantic errors. In many tales available to Shakespeare, a disguised woman inspires another woman's unhappy love. Most such stories were Italian, influenced by classical models, like Ovid's *Iphis*. The Italian tales, like their English prose counterparts, imitate the droll Ovidian manner of sexual innuendo. *As You Like It* and *Twelfth Night* depart from their sources in avoiding bedchamber intrigue. Shakespeare is interested in psychology not pornography.'[30]

James I (1566-1625)

James I was the only son of Mary Queen of Scots. In 1587 his mother was executed for treason. James was eager to succeed Elizabeth I so he did not protest much: he went to Scandinavia and brought his bride Anne of Denmark back to England in 1589. Anne bore him several children but she irritated him by becoming a Roman Catholic. In 1603 James I was the first Stuart to be crowned king of England. His reign included the Guy Fawkes conspiracy in 1605 and discontent between the Church of England and the Catholics.

James' counsellors were Robert Carr and George Villiers. George Villiers was introduced to King James to lessen the hold of Robert Carr and the Howard clan. James pronounced Villiers to be his "greatest love" and remained "sole monarch in the king's affection." In 1619 Queen Anne died. James was dispirited and fell severely ill with the gout. Buckingham took care of James, and their love deepened intensely. In 1620 James arranged for the political marriage of Buckingham to Lady Catherine Manners. James dissolved Parliament in 1621, 4 years later he was dead.

Philippe I Duc d'Orléans (1640-1701)

Philippe was the younger brother of Louis XIV. His mother, Anne of Austria, dressed him as a girl and neglected his education to discourage any rivalry between her sons. Philippe married twice and produced heirs.

He married Henriette Anne, sister of his cousin Charles II, in 1661, and had two daughters. Henriette was very close to the king of France. This made Philippe jealous; the final straw was when Henriette conspired with Louis to banish Philippe's lover the Chevalier de Lorraine from court. Henriette died unexpectedly in 1670 and Philippe was suspected of having her poisoned.

In 1671, he married the German princess Charlotte Elisabeth who bore him a son and daughter. The most infamous homosexual in France was the father of four children and a member of The Sacred Fraternity of Glorious Pederasts. This fraternity chose to ignore women, granting them the privilege of producing heirs and that was all. Their medallion depicted a man stepping on a woman and their meetings included performing fellatio. In 1701 he died after a fit of apoplexy.

Sir Isaac Newton (1642-1727)

Sir Isaac Newton is considered the scientific genius of the seventeenth century. Newton and his mother forged a close bond when his father died soon after Isaac's birth. When she remarried 3 years later, Isaac was left in the care of his grandmother. The child resented every minute he was away from his mother. Newton's stepfather died in 1656 allowing Newton and his mother to reunite. While at school he was a friend of Anne Storey, the stepdaughter of his landlord.

He attended Trinity College, Cambridge, in 1661. In 1665 the University was closed due to the plague; so students were dismissed and worked on their own. These events turned an irresolute scholar into a dynamo-thinking machine. He laid the foundations for differential and integral calculus. Newton's discoveries so impressed his teacher, Isaac Barrow, that he recommended the 27-year-old Newton replace him.

Newton's sexuality is controversial. Some believe he died a virgin, while others point to one big, gay love affair with Fatio de Duillier, a handsome, young Swiss mathematician.

'The two men were inseparable companions for several years, starting in 1687, when Fatio was 23. They shared a burning interest in Science and mathematics. Whether they also shared a bed is speculation. Newton and Fatio broke off their relationship in 1693. They exchanged occasional letters for the rest of their lives, but the friendship remained distant. For the next 18 months Newton suffered a complete nervous breakdown.'[31]

Installed in his London home was Catherine Barton, Newton's niece. Whether or not they were involved is hard to tell but it is assumed that Newton encouraged her affair with Montague to ensure Newton's appointment as master of the mint.

In *Principia* (1687) he explained the laws of motion and universal gravitation. *Principia* is recognised as the greatest scientific writing ever produced. After it was published he suffered a nervous breakdown. 'He lived in the world of the mind, often simply forgetting to sleep or eat.'[32]

Queen Anne knighted him in 1708. He was the first scientist to be so honoured.

Voltaire (1694-1778)

Voltaire claimed to have had a miserable childhood and believed his real father was the Abbé de Châteauneuf. The Abbé paid for a Jesuit education for Voltaire. Voltaire became a writer and by his early twenties he was the toast of Paris. His books sold and his plays were well attended. Yet by the time he was 30 Voltaire had already had lengthy affairs with perhaps a dozen women, including the Duchess de Villars, wife of the Marshal of France, and the famous actress Adrienne Lecouvreur. His homosexual liaisons occurred in his late twenties in Paris.

His literary success was founded in his passionate political beliefs, which raised all kinds of questions and infuriated authority. Advocating such radical causes as inoculation against disease, religious tolerance, trial by jury and the right of a people to choose its rulers, Voltaire flaunted the royal censors, his sometime patron Frederick the Great of Prussia and his good friend Louis XV. Voltaire spent much of his life in danger of arrest or exile. An avid Anglophile, he often took refuge in England, where he made friends with Pope and Congreve.[33]

Throughout his life, whether in France or 'resting/writing' in Vevey, Switzerland, Voltaire was the destination of many visitors.[34] His 'divine mistress' and translator was the Marquise de Châtelet, Emilie le Tonnelier de Breteuil. They were together from 1733 for 16 years until she died in childbirth while having an affair with another poet, the Marquis de Saint-Lambert. The Marquise and Voltaire had ceased sexual relations but still lived together. His niece stepped in as housekeeper, lover and confidante after her death. She was accused of material motives but she took care of him until the end of his life.

Marie-Antoinette (1755-1793)

Marie-Antoinette's lesbian antics were parodied in cartoons of the time, but her husband, Louis (the King of France) remained devoted to her. Marie-Antoinette was the daughter of Maria Theresa of Austria and Francis I, the Holy Roman Emperor. She is generally regarded as the linchpin for the French revolution though her behaviour was probably no worse than any other aristocrat of the period.

She married Louis in 1770. He assumed the throne as Louis XVI in 1774. Popular opinion painted her as a treacherous foreigner but her acceptance swayed back and forth. After the birth of her son, Louis Joseph, in 1778 her image improved.

The Affair of the Diamond Necklace left her reputation in tatters. The Comtesse de la Motte was a con woman and acquired a necklace from Cardinal de Rohan disguised as Marie-Antoinette. She duped the cleric, purloined the jewels and sent them to England. Marie-Antoinette had nothing to do with the affair but she was blamed until the countess was caught, the cardinal banished and the jewels recovered. The Flight to Varennes sealed her fate and she was found guilty of treason and beheaded in 1793.

'The Renaissance court aesthetic is still thriving in the eighteenth century, when Pope denounces Lord Hervey as a cynical court hermaphrodite and Mirabeau calls Marie-Antoinette "the only man at court."'[35]

Napoléon Bonaparte (1769-1821)

Napoléon's military career was unexciting until the capture of Toulon in 1793. Toulon was held by the British and French Royalists; this success earned him a heads up back in Paris from the Republic. His military triumphs continued until he executed a coup d'etat in 1799 and became master of France at 30. He abdicated in 1814 and by 1815 was exiled to Elba. Napoléon married Joséphine, the Creole mistress of Count Paul Barras. When the marriage proved fruitless, Napoléon married the 18-year-old Marie-Louise of Austria. Their son was born a year after the marriage. Napoléon had many mistresses and homosexual badinage with those who served him.

'Napoléon not only tolerated homosexuality among his associates; he also refused to permit punitive legislation against its practice. His habit of caressing his soldiers intimately while tweaking noses or pulling ears hinted strongly at his own homosexuality. Aides were often chosen for their youth and effeminate behaviour. To one, Napoléon gave the nickname "Miss Sainte Croix." Another, the baron Gaspard Gourgard, was the emperor's personal orderly for 6 years. Gourgard was furiously jealous of any that dared pay undue personal attention to "Her Majesty," his affectionate name for his master.'[36]

35

Frederick II (1712-1786)

Frederick II of Prussia had a miserable childhood. His father beat him in public. Frederick William I wanted to make Frederick a soldier. When Frederick had enough, he and his friend Lieutenant Katte tried to escape the King's tyranny by leaving for England. They were arrested and Frederick was forced to witness the execution of Lieutenant Katte.

In 1740 Frederick assumed the responsibilities of leading Prussia, placating his father by studying and commanding a regiment. He succeeded with full qualifications in kingcraft. Before his father's death Frederick married Elizabeth Christine, the daughter of a Prussian noble, in 1733. Frederick tried to provide an heir but without much success. Aided by Voltaire's visits to the Prussian court, Frederick's reputation was defined as homosexual.

However, Frederick also had encounters with women, so he was more probably bisexual. When his father died, Frederick II opened the court to writers from Berlin and invaded Silesia. Frederick was considered an example of enlightened despotism. He concentrated on rebuilding the war-ravaged territories which made up Prussia. He also banned torture, allowed some freedom of the press, religious toleration except for Jews and codified the Prussian laws.

Casanova (1725-1798)

Giovanni Casanova was born in 1725 to a Venetian actress Zanetta Farussi and a dancer named Casanova. He was expelled from a military academy for a homosexual relationship at 17 and exchanged love tokens with the ravishingly handsome Russian Lieutenant Lunin. As a youth his enthusiasm landed him in trouble with gender identification. Casanova believed he was having a wild affair with castrati named Bellino, who turned out to be a girl who wanted to be a singer.

He studied homeopathy and this talent encouraged Matteo Bragadin, an older man, to adopt him. Bragadin and Casanova were rumoured to have had a sexual relationship. Casanova was incarcerated for sexual 'peccadilloes' and then wandered around Europe for 18 years when he escaped. Women were crazy for him. He enjoyed bedding pairs of women. He seduced with foreplay, bathing and caressing his conquests until, all riled up, they let it happen. Casanova enjoyed performing sexually to satisfy voyeurs as in the case of 'mother mm' a nun, whose lover the Abbé François de Bernis observed Casanova and the nun stir it up.

Casanova was bisexual and could be enchanted by men and women. He was also a lawyer, writer, traveller and a member of the occult. He wrote extensively about his adventures and preferred quality to quantity in his sexual escapades. He enjoyed the seduction as much as the act and was experienced in many life disciplines, which probably contributed to his reputation as an exquisite lover.

Histoire De Ma Vie took twelve volumes to chronicle his marathon of a life. Casanova joined the Venetian army where he was imprisoned for sexual wrongdoing but managed to escape. Then he organised the French Lottery, translated the *Iliad* and visited Voltaire. He fought a duel with a Polish count and interviewed Catherine the Great about calendar reform. He was a spy for the Inquisition until he was exiled for writing a satire on the privileged of Venice in 1781.

Marquis de Sade (1740-1814)

The Marquis de Sade's name is synonymous with violence and sexuality of a brutal variety.

His father was glad to get him married off but the choice of family was a little too powerful for the shenanigans that the Marquis was going to get up to. His in-laws were the prestigious family of Montreuil, who had the ear of the monarchy and the court. De Sade liked orgies and he spent a good deal of time organising and participating in them. He also spent a good deal of time in prison.

It is not surprising that de Sade suffered from venereal disease. What did he do? Specifically, he hired and debauched professional women and amateurs, sodomised and whipped them, feeding them bon-bons in between.

In 1763, the marquis enticed Jeanne Testard to his house. He invited her to whip him and choose a whip for herself so he could return the favour. He forced her to destroy a crucifix and then she left. For this he received 15 days.

In 1768 he picked up Rose Keller and beat her, intermittently rubbing salve on her lacerations. De Sade's family bribed her into silence but she had already reported his actions to the police. The police arrested him as an example of the depraved aristocracy. When Renée Pélagie, his wife, visited him he managed to get her pregnant again. Having accomplished this he was paroled and told to go and live quietly on his estate in the south of France.

At the Château of La Coste the Marquis, his sister in law, Anne Prospère, and Renée had a lively winter. Orgies were staged with four prostitutes from Marseilles. De Sade and his valet, Latour, beat, had anal sex and vaginal intercourse with all the ladies. An earlier participant had too much Spanish fly and was found vomiting uncontrollably. De Sade and Latour fled the city but were judged in their absence and executed in effigy.

De Sade was caught and jailed in Sardinia but escaped and lived as a fugitive. When he returned, Renée was waiting for him and they began to concoct more mischief. This time they enlisted a procuress and hired five 15-year-old girls and a small boy. Returning to Paris because his mother was sick, de Sade was arrested under the Lettre de Cachet taken out by his mother-in-law. De Sade was imprisoned for 12 and a half years in 1777.

While in prison he developed two more talents: writing and masturbating. He wrote other books besides erotica but he is mainly recalled for his 'sadism' and the novel *Justine*.

De Sade was released from prison by the revocation of the monarchist power of imprisonment by Lettre de Cachet during the French Revolution. 'He was now Citizen Sade, a pamphleteer, orator and a living legend for having incited, from his tower cell, the historic storming of the Bastille.'[37]

He became a revolutionary judge and was nearly guillotined for being too moderate when he hesitated in condemning his mother-in-law to the guillotine. In 1801 he was in trouble again, this time with Napoléon and his wife Joséphine who were piqued at a pamphlet lampooning them. Napoléon said it was for the content of *Justine* but some knew otherwise.

De Sade finished his life in Charenton asylum. He staged dramas at the asylum and had several lovers nearby: Renée Pélagie and Catherine Trillet (aka Justine). De Sade inspired loyalty in his women and servants.

Lord Byron (1788-1824)

George Gordon was born with a clubfoot and inherited the title Lord Byron at the age of 10. At that age, Byron was initiated sexually by his nurse who was a frequent visitor to his bed. Byron watched her perform uninhibited sex with her lovers. At Harrow, he preferred young boys: the Earl of Clare, the Duke of Dorset; and John Edleston (they sealed their commitment with a heart-shaped carnelian at parting).

To overcome his disability he became a competitive swimmer. But this did not win his battle with obesity. He ate soda crackers, took drugs and fasted all to no avail. After scandals in London with two mistresses (one disguised as a boy, who miscarried at a hotel in Bond Street, and the other as a cousin), he set out on a two-year tour of Europe.

Upon his return in 1812 he presented *Childe Harold's Pilgrimage* a poem of Spenserien stanzas. Byron enjoyed immediate success with this poem. He met Lady Caroline Lamb, the uninhibited wife of future Prime Minister William Lamb, Lord Melbourne. Caroline and Byron became lovers but her erratic behaviour discouraged him and so they parted.

Childe Harold's Pilgrimage was followed by *The Bride Of Abydos And The Corsair* (1814, sold 10,000 copies the first day) and *The Siege Of Corinth*. In July 1813 Byron had an incestuous relationship with his half-sister Augusta Leigh. Byron married Annabella Milbanke to silence the chorus of disapproval that greeted his pleasure in the birth of Medora, Augusta's and his daughter. Annabella was grim and thought she would reform him. It lasted a year as Byron tormented her with tales or orgies and fornication. To her total disgust he would not allow her to touch him. As Annabella sought a legal separation the charges against Byron were increased: raping a thirteen-year-old and sodomising his wife in the final month of her pregnancy. Annabella had a resolute supporter in Lady Caroline Lamb who had been spurned by Byron after a brief, passionate affair.

Byron was forced to leave England for good in April 1816. In this year he published *The Prisoner Of Chillon*. He took up residence in Venice around the corner from St Mark's Square. His landlady Marianne Segati and the baker's wife Margarita Cogni became his mistresses. His relentless partying caused the two mistresses to behave erratically. Marianne was dismissed in 1818 and Byron rented the Palazzo Mocenigo. Margarita had one temper tantrum too many. She threatened him with a knife, stabbed him in the hand and jumped into the canal.

Once Margarita was fully convinced that Byron was over her she returned to her husband. He estimated great expense was incurred for whores and the treatment of his gonorrhoea. In 1819, Byron met Teresa Guiccioli, a 19-year-old countess trapped in a marriage of convenience. (He also began work on *Don Juan* and did not finish it before his death.) He escorted her socially but then fell in love with her. Teresa was granted a legal separation and they lived together until Byron left for Greece and died.

'Byron became certain that actions were more important than writing books and so he bought a ship and sailed to Greece to help the effort there. He died of a fever before he saw any fighting. Byron was the greatest Romantic poet and satirist. His unfinished masterpiece *Don Juan* was universally acknowledged as a lyrical masterpiece and satirical oeuvre. He was famous for love affairs with women and Mediterranean boys.'[38]

George Sand (1804-1876)

George Sand was the pseudonym of Aurore Dudevant. Sand is recognised as the most influential French female writer of the nineteenth century. She was married at 18 and had two children but it was an unhappy marriage (Casimir Dudevant occasionally beat her and was a drunk) so she left in 1831. She moved to Paris with another man and wrote to support her family.

Her novels include *Indiana, Valentine, Lelia, The Companion Of The Tour Of France*, her memoirs *My Life, Consuelo, The Countess Of Rudolstadt, The Haunted Pool* and *The Country Waif*. She was a pamphleteer during the 1848 uprisings and retired to her country estate at Nohant when the return of Napoléon III plunged her into despair.

George Sand adopted male dress and behaved in a masculine fashion. She was linked to the actress Marie Dorval but she also had male lovers including Alfred de Musset and Frederic Chopin. 'She was short and swarthy, with heavy features and dark eyes. Her manner was brusque. In her intellect and passion for living lay her sensual appeal.'[39]

Her ideas and her manner of writing enlivened the hopes of women, though Sand's work did not become available in English translation until the twentieth century. According to Camille Paglia, George Sand inspired Balzac's androgynous characters in *The Human Comedy* and *Cousin Bette*, also the 1835 painting *Mademoiselle de Maupin* by Théophile Gautier, now considered a masterpiece.

Peter Ilyich Tchaikovsky (1840-1893)

Tchaikovsky was a leading Russian composer of the nineteenth century. He is considered the master composer of classical ballet. His ballet *The Nutcracker* is performed all over the world at Christmas time, though he considered it inferior to his *Sleeping Beauty, Swan Lake, Romeo And Juliet* and *The 1812 Overture* are all staples of classical music and are enjoyed by concert-goers internationally.

Alternating between periods of elated composition and nervous breakdowns, Tchaikovsky finally married a student of his. She was a nymphomaniac. His attempted suicide disentangled him from the marriage and secured an annuity from a wealthy patroness, which enabled him to give up teaching and spend his life composing and travelling. He was gay, as was his brother, Modeste. He wrote to his brother, 'Only now, especially after the story of my marriage, have I finally begun to understand that there is nothing more fruitless than not wanting to be that which I am by nature.'

Tchaikovsky fell hopelessly in love with his nephew 'Bob.' 'Bob will finally drive me simply crazy with his indescribable fascination... I begin to crave Bob and get lonely without him... Frightful how I love him!' The overwhelming anguish this caused led Tchaikovsky to compose his famous Symphony #6, the *Pathétique*. Within a week of its first performance, Tchaikovsky was dead.

Paul Verlaine (1844-1896)

Verlaine was the son of a prosperous army officer. His mother was a little eccentric - she kept the foetuses of her three stillborn infants in glass jars. Indulging every whim of her weak and irresponsible son, by the age of 13 or 14 he was 'overcome with sensuality'; he was attracted to young boys and described Lucien Viotti as having 'an exquisitely proportioned body.' Then he discovered the pleasures of female prostitutes, alcohol and absinthe. *Poemes Saturniens* was his first volume of verse published in

1866. Verlaine was able to translate visuals into words and his eloquence captured paintings and music. In 1870 he married Mathilde Maute.

Verlaine had a civil service job, which was interrupted by the Franco-Prussian war and the arrival of Arthur Rimbaud in Paris in 1871. *La Bonne Chanson* (1870), *Romances Sans Paroles* (1874) and *Sagesse* (1881) are some of his most important collections of poetry. His later work is not considered as communicative.

Rimbaud turned Verlaine's life upside down. At the end of the two-year affair Verlaine was in jail for 18 months for having assaulted Rimbaud. Verlaine turned to religion while in jail. He became a sexual vagabond drifting from one partner to another. Some relationships were violent, others penitent; on occasion he returned to live with his mother where he wrote. After her death he lived in public hospitals being catered to and treated as a celebrity.

Oscar Wilde (1854-1900)

The sexuality of Oscar Wilde gave rise to one of the most infamous trials in history. 'Infamous' because Wilde's imprisonment resulted in *The Ballad Of Reading Gaol*. It is a poem laced with gruelling description of the horrors of British prisons at the end of the nineteenth century. His brilliance was to turn that horrendous experience into an epic call to reform the conditions in the British prison system. His Crime? 'Wilde was charged with and tried for homosexual practices, found guilty, and sentenced to two years' imprisonment with hard labour. By the time he was released he was broken, both as an artist and as a man. Wilde was found guilty of committing specific acts abhorrent by the moral standards of the time. Our culture, in its collective and selective memory, translates those acts into an image of an exclusively homosexual man, despite Wilde's active sexual pursuit of women well into his early thirties.'[40]

Wilde was born in Dublin and dressed as a girl by his mother who longed for a daughter. His mother was a patriotic Irish poet. Oscar's father, Sir William Wilde, was involved in a sensational trial. He was famous as a doctor and an intellectual, and was accused of having violated a woman patient.

Oscar was awarded scholarships for all his university education. He attended Trinity College, Dublin, from 1871 to 1874. He won the Berkeley Gold Medal for Greek and was awarded the prestigious Newdigate Prize for his poem *Ravenna* in 1878 by Magdalen College, Oxford. After university, he moved to London with his friend, Frank Miles, a well-known and socially connected painter.

In 1881 he published his first collection of poems: *POEMS*. It was well received and in December he sailed for America. His lecture series was entitled *The Aesthetics*. The 50-city 4-month tour stretched to a year and he delivered 140 lectures in 260 days. While in America, he met Henry Longfellow, Oliver Wendell Holmes and Walt Whitman. Then he lectured in Britain and Ireland.

In 1884, Oscar married Constance Lloyd who was bright and spoke several languages. For two years they were deeply in love and had two sons Cyril (1885) and Vyvyan (1886). With a family to support, Oscar accepted an editorial position to launch a periodical called *The Woman's World*. In 1890 Oscar's first play, *The Picture Of Dorian Gray*, opened. It was very successful in terms of moral outrage but produced little money. During this time he wrote some children's stories: *The Happy Prince And Other Tales* in 1888 and *The House Of Pomegranates* in 1892.

Oscar suffered a recurrence of syphilis contracted from a prostitute while at college. He had consulted a doctor before proposing to Constance and had been reassured that he was cured. When the disease flared up again, he ceased having sexual relations with Constance. At that time the only treatment for syphilis was mercury which caused the discoloration of the teeth and Oscar's teeth were already seriously discoloured by the mercury treatments from his initial cure. He turned his attention from Constance to boys.

In the summer of 1891 he met 'Bosie' (Lord Alfred Douglas) the great love of his life. Bosie's father did not like Wilde and, after insulting Wilde at his club, Wilde took him to court in April 1895 and lost. The counter-suit accused Wilde of consorting with young men. Rent boys were paraded into court to testify about the details of their sexual intimacy with Oscar Wilde.

Wilde was sentenced to two years' hard labour. Constance took the children to Switzerland. *The Ballad Of Reading Gaol* was published before Constance's death in 1898. He wandered through Europe visiting friends and writing the occasional article for Parisian papers. Wilde spent time with Bosie and then died in November 1900.

Sigmund Freud (1856-1939)

Sigmund Freud wrote: 'To undertake to convert a fully developed homosexual into a heterosexual does not offer much more prospect for success than the reverse, except that for good practical reasons the latter is never attempted.'

Freud's writing and establishment of the methods of psychoanalysis have affected the way sex is discussed and understood. He was the oldest and favourite of 8 children. Freud attended the University of Vienna and took 8 years to graduate because he couldn't decide what subject to pursue. At the age of 30 he married Martha Bernays. They had 9 children and Martha took care of all the details of Freud's routine and life.

Freud wrote: 'Homosexuality is assuredly no advantage, but it is nothing to be ashamed of, no vice, no degradation, it cannot be classified as an illness... It is a great injustice to persecute homosexuality as a crime, and cruelty too.'

Freud had a significant relationship with Dr Wilhelm Fleiss. They met in 1887, when Fleiss, who was an ear, nose and throat specialist, attended one of Freud's lectures in Vienna on neuropathology. Their friendship ended due to a disagreement as to who owned the intellectual property in their correspondence and work on bisexuality. At first Freud rejected the idea, then claimed it as his own, and planned to write a major book on it, giving Fleiss only minimal credit. Freud came to believe in a strong bisexual aspect to every personality and wrote, 'Every sex act is one between four individuals.'[43]

'In the context of these ideas, and in an intellectual climate that had already produced speculations on homosexuality as a third sex by sexologists like Richard von Krafft-Ebing, Havelock Ellis and Magnus Hirschfield, the concept of bisexuality, and of what Freud in his early papers began to call the bisexual disposition of all human beings, seems far from extreme.'[41]

'To the end of his life Freud wrestled with the "conundrum" of bisexuality. It might indeed be said that he came back after death as what he liked to call a "revenant" to offer some final views, for in the posthumously published *Outline Of Psycho-Analysis* (1938) he returned once again to "the great enigma of the biological fact of the duality of the sexes."'[42]

Havelock Ellis (1859-1939)

Havelock Ellis was not a bisexual but his contribution to the sexual dialogue was enhanced by his seven-volume work: *Studies In The Psychology Of Sex* written between 1897 and 1928.

Havelock was the son of a sea captain and an indulgent mother. He grew up in Croydon and attended private school in London. A sea voyage to Australia restored his poor health and while there he worked as a teacher. Upon his return to London he attended St Thomas' Hospital. When he graduated, he practised medicine for a time and finally decided to pursue a literary career. His first book *The New Spirit* was published when he was 30 and, though he continued writing and publishing his work, he had little success until *The Dance Of Life* when he was 64.

Havelock Ellis married Edith Lees who was manic-depressive and a lesbian. Their sex life suffered as a result. Edith reprimanded Havelock for falling in love with the 24-year-old daughter of a chemist friend. In 1916 Edith died in a diabetic coma. Havelock met and became enchanted with Margaret Sanger, the birth control crusader. Margaret found him a 'Tall angel, blue-eyed, handsome, with a distinctive flowing white beard.'[44]

Havelock cured his impotence in 1918 with the help of Françoise Cyon's loving attention. After a turbulent start to their relationship, Françoise and Havelock finally enjoyed 22 years together. During his lifetime, Ellis defended homosexuals and women's rights, and pioneered open discussions on sex. He gave free advice on sex to anyone who wanted it and could not understand why Freud charged patients for the same help. Ellis was a sweet and humane man, part scientist and part mystic.

André Gide (1869-1951)

André Gide is considered a titan of French literature. He was born in Paris to a prominent family. Unfortunately, he lost his father when he was very young and his mother was overprotective. Expelled from school for masturbating in class, his mother took him to the doctor who threatened to castrate him if he did not desist. Gide was slow to have any sexual experiences with other people. He had his first sexual encounter at the age of 23 in the arms of a 14-year-old Tunisian boy.

In 1893, Gide, Oscar Wilde and Bosie met in Algiers; Wilde procured a musician called Mohammad for Gide, who recalled it as the ultimate sexual experience. He formed a close attachment with his 15-year-old servant boy, Athman, and brought him to Paris after wrangling with his mother for years about whether he should bring him or not. Gide married his cousin, Madeleine Rondeaux, after his mother died. For the rest of his life he worshipped her but Gide suffered from 'angelism,' a condition where the sufferer is unable to accomplish sexual interaction with the beloved. Madeleine had to be content with a platonic friendship with her husband.[45]

At 46, Gide had a heterosexual affair with Elizabeth van Rysselberghe resulting in the birth of a daughter Catherine. Gide acknowledged the child and lived to be a grandfather. At 47, Gide fell in love with Marc, the 16-year-old son of a friend, who had attended Gide's wedding. The love affair matured into an enduring friendship.

Gide earned the respect of his peers by discussing homosexuality frankly at a time when such discussion was prohibited. His books shocked the public and upset his wife. The Catholic Church banned his literary works. At the age of 78, Oxford University and a Nobel Prize awarded him a doctorate for Literature. André Gide openly acknowledged his homosexuality in *The Immoralist* and *The Counterfeiters*.

Sidonie Gabrielle Colette (1873-1954)

Colette was the author of 73 books in a career that spanned 54 years. She married three times in her life. The first was Henry Gauthier Villars, 35-year-old writer and friend of the family. Henry encouraged Colette to write her fantasies, resulting in the 4 best-selling Claudine books and Willy, as Henry was known, marketed them to death. There were, for example, Claudine soaps and cosmetics. Willy was unfaithful and enticed

Colette to have threesomes with his mistresses. Colette rebelled against Willy, who had signed his name to her work. She began to perform in cabaret and appeared in diaphanous scarves baring everything for art. Colette divorced Willy in 1906 and found her own friends, including Missy, the former Marquise de Belboeuf, who dressed like a man and lived with Collete after the divorce. Colette had many lesbian lovers including Natalie Barney and Polaire, an actress.

Henry de Jouvenel was the editor of *Le Matin*, her second husband and father of her only daughter. In 1920, *Chéri* was published. It is the story of an ageing flirt and a young gigolo. *The Ripening Seed* (1923) is a coming-of-age tale. In 1935 she married journalist Maurice Goudeket and in 1945 wrote *Gigi* when she was 72.

Gigi catapulted her to international acclaim when her best-selling book was made into a top-grossing musical that enthralled audiences and earned the praise of the most jaundiced of critics. She became one of the most famous French novelists read by fans around the world.

W Somerset Maugham (1874-1965)

W Somerset Maugham wrote *Of Human Bondage*, *The Moon And Sixpence*, *The Razor's Edge* and many short stories. Maugham spoke French and English having been raised in Paris. His father was the solicitor for the British embassy. His parents died by the time he was ten and the young boy was sent to a clergyman's house (his father's brother). He attended King's School in Canterbury and developed a stammer. His health was frail and so he went to Heidelberg University in Germany. He began to write and completed his first novel, *Liza Of Lambeth*, at the age of 23.

He turned to playwriting and soon had 4 hit plays on stage in London. By the age of 41 he had concluded his biographical masterpiece *Of Human Bondage*. In Heidelberg he had his first homosexual experience. When he returned to London he dared not risk homosexual practices for the Oscar Wilde trial was only two years old, so he consorted with women. His conquests included: feminist Violet Hunt, who edited *The Freewoman*; Sasha Kropotkin, daughter of the Russian anarchist; and Ethelwyn Jones aka Sue Jones who inspired the character of Rosie in his novel *Cakes And Ale*. Maugham proposed to Sue but she was pregnant by another man, turned him down and married the 6th Earl of Antrim.

Instead, he married Syrie Barnardo Wellcome and she was a heap of trouble. She was enthusiastic about sex with Maugham and he wasn't. His patronising attitude is reflected in this letter to her: 'I married you because I thought it the best thing for your happiness and for [their daughter] Elizabeth's welfare, but I did not marry you because I loved you, and you were only too well aware of that.' Contrary to his belief as to what was best for her, Syrie became a successful interior designer.

Maugham met his life love in France during World War One. Gerald Haxton was born in San Francisco but raised in Britain. For 30 years Maugham looked after Gerald, whose only desire out of life was 'fun and games.' They travelled a great deal and Gerald was personable and useful to Maugham. Gerald served as Maugham's secretary/companion and was a competent procurer. Boys from Mexico and Indochina kept Maugham's love life spicy.

After the death of Gerald Haxton, Alan Searle replaced him. Alan Searle was a sweet, kind ex-social worker who adored Maugham. Maugham tried to adopt him but was sued by his daughter Elizabeth when a part of the adoption involved disowning her. Maugham lived to be 92.

Gertrude Stein (1874-1946) & Alice B Toklas

These ladies were not bisexual but their inclusion is necessary for they fostered many heterosexual, bisexual, homosexual and lesbian artist and writers.

Gertrude Stein was convinced of her own genius. As a child she lived in Vienna and Paris before returning to settle in Oakland, California. Her mother died and Gertrude was harassed into studying medicine. She studied Psychology at Radcliffe College and John Hopkins where she flunked out due to an identity crisis brought on by her first lesbian affair. She moved to Paris funded by her parents' money. Gertrude and Leo, her art dealer brother, shared an apartment. They collected Cubist paintings. They not only bought and collected paintings but painters too! Picasso, Braque and Matisse were in their circle of friends. Gertrude wrote *Q.E.D.* in 1903 (not published until 1950), *Three Lives* (1909) which was well received by the critics, and *The Making Of Americans* (not published until 1925).

In autumn of 1907, Gertrude met Alice B Toklas, 'a well-heeled gal' from San Francisco 'doing Europe.' Gertrude invited Alice to move in and she did. She proof-read one of Gertrude's books.

Gertrude and Alice entered into a married relationship where Alice took care of the details and Gertrude was free to write and work as she desired. Their partnership lasted until 1946 when Gertrude died after cancer surgery. Alice lived another 21 years heartsick and lonely still missing her Gertrude. Gertrude wrote Alice's biography which was in fact her own, so entwined in each other's lives had they become. It was a perfect Sapphic love story.

The Bloomsbury Group

In 1904, there was a tea party in Bloomsbury, London, hosted by Vanessa and Virginia Stephen. Lytton Strachey (biographer of Queen Elizabeth and Queen Victoria), was present and from this first meeting developed a group of artists who brought about a renaissance in sexual mores by writing frankly and conclusively about all sorts of sexuality. They flouted convention and by so doing helped drag the British Empire from the reign of Victoria into the twentieth century.

Carstairs, Dolly Wilde, Connie Collier and Beatrice Lillie provided entrees in London. Lady Ottoline Morrell was a Duke's sister, a colourful personage, and the Bloomsbury set's most formidable bisexual hostess.[46]

Gatherings were held on Thursday evenings. They were attended "for whiskey, buns, cocoa and conversation"[47] Members of the group included Victoria Sackville-West and John Maynard Keynes (who became the most influential economist of his time). Vanessa Stephen married Clive Bell, who scandalised London by holding an exhibition of post-impressionist painters with his friend Roger Fry. Her sister Virginia married Leonard Woolf, an elegant and respected author who made the Hogarth Press into a major publishing enterprise.

Other members included author EM Forster, the painters Duncan Grant and Vanessa Bell, and GE Moore, the Cambridge author and philosopher of *Principia Ethica*, was their mentor. Virginia Woolf was the leader of this artistic universe. There were many bisexuals amongst them and they produced an enormous body of work that influenced the course of history.[48]

Virginia Woolf (1882-1941)

Virginia Woolf is considered one of the major writers of the twentieth century. She was the daughter of Julia Duckworth, a great beauty, and Sir Leslie Stephen, one of Britain's leading literary figures. Her half-brothers, Gerald and George Duckworth, took advantage of her sexually and she endured this humiliating treatment until she was 22. In later life, although Virginia flirted with men, she gave her heart to women. She endured periods of madness brought on by the stress of completing books, until aged 59, during another lunatic episode, she filled her pockets with stones and drowned in the River Ouse.

The Bloomsbury group developed when her brothers' Cambridge friends descended upon their London house and used it as a headquarters for their meetings and debates. Madge Vaughan was one of her lady friends, replaced (when she married) by Violet Dickinson.

Virginia did not marry until she was 30. Lytton Strachey proposed to her in 1909 but then recanted his proposal and inserted Leonard Woolf to court Virginia's affections. (Lytton Strachey was a gay man but he too married for social acceptance.) Virginia and Leonard were happily married, but they had a frigid sex life. At the age of 40, Virginia's life was changed when she met the 30-year-old lesbian Vita Sackville-West. *The Death Of The Moth*, *Orlando*, *Mrs Dalloway*, *The Waves* and *To The Lighthouse* were written during the time of her affair with Vita. Harold Nicolson called *Orlando*, 'the longest and most charming love letter in history.'

Vita Sackville-West (1892-1962)

Vita was educated privately and her first poetry was written as a child. By the age of 18, she produced several novels published in the 1910s. In 1913 she married the diplomat and critic Harold Nicolson.

'Harold Nicolson had affairs with men throughout his married life. The Painter Duncan Grant was the lover of economist John Maynard Keynes for more than 6 years. Then Grant had an affair with Virginia Woolf's brother Adrian; he spent the remainder of his life in a ménage à trois with Woolf's artist sister Vanessa Bell and the writer David Garnett. Keynes... was an active and enthusiastic homosexual who was considered by his

Bloomsbury friends to be "married" to Grant before his own heterosexual marriage to ballerina Lydia Lopokova.'[49]

Vita's other lifelong companion was Violet Trefusis, the daughter of Alice Keppel, Edward VII's mistress. They had met as children, later eloped to France and had to be lured home by their husbands. *Challenge And Her Diaries* were inspired by this relationship with Violet.

Beautiful and talented, Vita was a successful poet, novelist and biographer, a shining member of the Bloomsbury group. Her poetry won prizes in 1926 and 1946 but was not as well regarded as her novels: *The Edwardians* (1930), *All Passion Spent* (1931) and *Pepita* (a fictionalised account of the life of her grandmother, a Spanish dancer). Her biographies included Aphra Behn and Saint Joan of Arc.

Victoria 'Vita' Sackville-West loved many women and a few men and had a knack for turning lovers into friends. Her physical liaison with Virginia Woolf was brief (in five years they slept together about a dozen times),[50] but their friendship lasted for the rest of their lives (Woolf's *Orlando* is said to be a portrait of West), although it almost broke up Vita's marriage to the diplomat Harold Nicolson.[51]

Vita's affair with Virginia Woolf's eldest sister, Vanessa Bell, the painter was short, but led Vanessa to paint innovative nudes. Everybody remembered Vanessa's 1931 masked party where Vita came as Sappho.[52]

Eleanor Roosevelt (1884-1962)

Eleanor Roosevelt was the wife of a president and an American humanitarian. She was born in New York City. The daughter of Elliott Roosevelt and niece of Theodore Roosevelt, she was an active worker in social causes before she married Franklin Delano Roosevelt, a distant cousin, in 1905. They had five children and were happy until, in 1918, the love letters of Lucy Mercer revealed her affair with Franklin. Eleanor called a family conference and the issue of the affair was debated. They decided to remain together but with a new understanding - Eleanor did not have to be faithful to her wedding vows.

When Franklin Roosevelt was stricken with poliomyelitis in 1921, Eleanor took a more active interest in public issues. She played a leading part in women's organisations, actively encouraged youth movements, promoted consumer welfare, worked for the civil rights of minorities and combated poor housing and unemployment.

'Roosevelt's friendships with two lesbian couples, Esther Lape and Elizabeth Read, and Nancy Cook and Marion Dickerman, developed during the 1920s. These relationships were part of a female support network that was social and cultural as well as political, which reminded Roosevelt of her years as a student at Madame Marie Souvestre's Allenwood School - years which... were to produce one of the most erotic "lesbian novels" of this century, Dorothy Strachey Bussy's *Olivia*.'[53]

She retained these interests after marriage and while rearing her five children. She had other passionate relationships: with Lorena Hickok (journalist) to whom she wrote over 2,300 letters; and Earl Miller (her former bodyguard and 13 years younger than her), a boxer, gymnast, swimmer, horseman and former acrobat.

'Her friends Nancy Cook and Marion Dickerman described the rumours that [Eleanor] Roosevelt had wanted to leave FDR after the 1932 election and marry Earl Miller.'[54]

In 1933, she conducted the first press conference ever held by a US president's wife. An accomplished writer, she initiated a daily column, My Day, in 1935 which was syndicated through the newspapers. She hosted a radio program and travelled around the country, lecturing, observing conditions and furthering causes. During World War Two she was assistant director of the Office of Civilian Defense (1941-42). She also visited Great Britain (1942), the South-West Pacific (1943) and the Caribbean (1944).

From 1945 to 1953 (and again in 1961) she was the American delegate to the United Nations, and in 1946 she was made chair of the Commission on Human Rights, a subsidiary of the UN Economic and Social Council. In the 1950s she became a leader of the liberal wing of the Democratic Party. Her dedication to the cause of human welfare won her affection and honour throughout the world as well as the respect of many of her critics. Many of her magazine and newspaper articles have been collected. Her other writings include *The Moral Basis Of Democracy* (1940) and *You Can Learn By Living* (1960).

'But the political energies that found it important to "reclaim" Eleanor Roosevelt for feminism and lesbianism have tended to regard the romance in her life as bound up with women, not with a woman and a man. To relabel her bisexual in a political way may be just to reshuffle the content of the boxes. Yet to fail to take cognisance of her capacity to have loving, erotic relationships, on paper and in person, with both men and women is, once again, to underestimate her qualities, her imagination and her remarkable will.'[55]

Waslaw Nijinsky (1890-1950)

Waslaw Nijinsky was born in Kiev in the Ukraine the son of two professional dancers. At the age of nine his father deserted the family for a pregnant mistress. His mother needed him to succeed and help feed the family. In 1907, he graduated from the St Petersburg Imperial School of Ballet and joined the Imperial Russian Ballet as a soloist. His career was spectacular. He danced in Paris and caused a sensation.

Nijinsky's love life was fraught with turmoil. His first sexual experience was homosexual at the hands of Prince Pavel Dmitrievich Lvov in 1908. Nijinsky was passive and not very well-endowed according to Prince Pavel. The prince treated him as a toy and arranged his first experience with a female prostitute, which repelled Waslaw. Before the prince abandoned Nijinsky he introduced him to Sergei Diaghilev, who was a complete homosexual and twenty years older than Nijinsky. Nijinsky did not enjoy sex with Diaghilev but endured it. Diaghilev took the opportunity of stripping Nijinsky of what little independence he had; he was not to consort with women. Isadora Duncan offered to have Nijinsky's baby in 1909 but he refused. In 1913, aboard the SS Avon, Nijinsky married 23-year-old Romola de Pulszky. Diaghilev fired Nijinsky for getting married.

Romola had a daughter in 1914 and another in 1920. At that point Diaghilev re-entered their lives and, although Romola sued him for 500,000 francs (the earnings that Nijinsky forfeited) and won the case, Diaghilev never paid. Unhinged by Diaghilev, Nijinsky was confined to Swiss asylums for the last 30 years of his life.

Edna St Vincent Millay (1892-1950)

Edna grew up in a remote town in Maine, America, the eldest daughter of a divorcee. She called herself Vincent and was the man of the house. Her mother was free-spirited and raised three daughters with a tight group of friends who were creative women. Vincent had a patron who paid for her education at Vassar when she was 21. As soon as she graduated, she moved to Greenwich Village. She was a great poet and won the Pulitzer Prize in 1923. Millay had an intoxicating effect on both men and women. In 1923 she married Eugen Boissevain who waited on her hand and foot for the 25 years of their marriage.

In *Great Companions*, Max Eastman relates an interesting story about Millay that, if true, reveals something of her attitude about her own sexuality. According to Eastman, while at a cocktail party Millay discussed her recurrent headaches with a psychologist. He asked her, "I wonder if it has ever occurred to you that you might perhaps, although you are hardly conscious of it, have an occasional impulse toward a person of your own sex?" She responded, "Oh, you mean I'm homosexual! Of course I am, and heterosexual too, but what's that got to do with my headache?"

In her own words: 'For surely, one must be either undiscerning, or frightened, to love only one person, when the world is so full of gracious and noble spirits.'

Djuna Chappell Barnes (1892-1982)

Djuna Chappell Barnes was born in Cornwall-on-Hudson, America, to a wealthy and free-spirited father, Henry Buddington Barnes, a painter/ farmer on Long Island, and his wife Elizabeth Chappell Barnes, an English violinist. Djuna and her 4 brothers and sisters were raised by her mother and suffragist grandmother. They were raised outside the school system. Her father was a great influence on her development as an artist. In 1911 she entered the Pratt Institute in Brooklyn.

After the divorce of her parents, she lived a Bohemian lifestyle in Greenwich Village and worked as a journalist and an illustrator. She married Courtenay Lemon, an editor, but it did not last long.[56] She interviewed fascinating characters like Frank Harris, Florenz Ziegfeld, DW Griffith and Diamond Jim Brady (they were published posthumously as *Interviews*). She was multi-talented: Barnes wrote poetry (*The Book Of*

Repulsive Women, 1915) and plays (she worked with Eugene O'Neill on several one-act plays at the Provincetown Playhouse).

From 1920, she spent 20 years abroad and interviewed Gertrude Stein, F Scott Fitzgerald, TS Eliot and James Joyce. In 1928, *Ladies Almanack* was banned by the United States' customs. *Ryder* followed in 1928. Next came *Nightwood* (1936). This was her triumph and drew intellectuals and writers to her including the patronage of Peggy Guggenheim. The story, set in Paris, is about the doomed lesbian relationship Robin Vote and Nora Flood. Nora has a transvestite doctor as her spiritual advisor. Djuna wrote over 20 more books and is sometimes referred to as the unknown legend of American literature. She ended her life quietly in New York and was inducted into the National Institute of Arts and Letters.

"'They're always referring to Djuna now as a lesbian, but she had many lovers, male and female," observed Djuna Barnes' friend, the poet Charles Henri Ford, who lived with Barnes in Paul Bowles' house in Tangier in 1933.'[57]

Anaïs Nin (1903-1977)

Born in Neuilly, France, Anaïs Nin went to the United States with her Danish mother and two brothers in 1914. Her father, Joaquin Nin, a Cuban-born composer and pianist, had seduced Nin in her childhood and abandoned the family when Anaïs was 11. In 1923 she married Hugh Guiler. He illustrated her books under the name Ian Hugo. They moved to Paris in the 1930s when Anaïs was writing fiction. Anaïs had a lively social and romantic life. Her liaison with Henry Miller was detailed in their correspondence, published in 1987 as *A Literary Passion*.

From 1931 to 1974 Anaïs Nin wrote journals. Using these *Journals* and *A Literary Passion*, a film was made called *Henry & June* (1992). It presents bisexual triangles within bigamous marriages: Henry Miller, June his wife, Anaïs Nin and her husband Hugo plus Anaïs' other husband Rupert Pole in Los Angeles. The film stars Maria de Medeiros in the part of Anaïs Nin and illustrates the jealousy involved within triangular situations. Just as June and Anaïs are about to get it on, Anaïs reveals that she has been sleeping with Henry and causes June to storm out.

"There are two facts that are very, very wrong and have to be corrected. One was that Anaïs Nin never, ever had a physical relationship with June

Miller. Anaïs Nin's first lesbian relationship happened during an orgy in the 1940s in New York City, and she didn't like it. And she never had a physical relationship with women after that. The second thing was that Hugh Guiler, her husband, was not the buffoon, the fool, the cuckold, the stupid, silly man that Phil Kaufman turned him into in that film. Hugh Guiler was an extremely sensitive, sophisticated man who knew everything that was going on but simply chose not to see it. So those two things notwithstanding, everything else in the film was pretty accurate."[58]

Her books include *D. H. Lawrence, An Unprofessional Study* (1932), *House Of Incest* (1936), *Under A Glass Bell* (1944) and more than 25 other titles. She was rediscovered in the 1960s - first estranged and then embraced by feminists.

Gertrude Ma Rainey (1886-1939)

Gertrude Pridgett was born on 26 April 1886 in Columbus, Georgia. Thomas and Ella Pridgett had been performers in minstrel shows and inspired Gertrude's interest in entertainment. Her stage career got its start with a song and dance troupe when she was only 14. In 1902, she heard her first blues song and adopted the style for her shows. Gertrude married travelling entertainer Will "Pa" Rainey in 1904. They toured as Ma & Pa Rainey and Assassinators of the Blues.

From humble beginnings, she went on to become the top recording artist for Paramount Records. Known as the "Mother of the Blues," she was also an outspoken bisexual both in her lyrics and her actions. Rainey put her money where her mouth was. The newspaper ad that promoted the release of 'Prove It On Me' featured Ma Rainey dressed in a man's suit flirting with two other women. She was outspoken on women's issues and was seen as a role model for future women entertainers who took control of their own careers. After 25 years of performing for her loyal fans, Rainey signed a recording contract in 1923. She released over 100 songs during a six-year recording career including: 'C.C. Rider' (or 'See See Rider'), 'Jellybean Blues,' 'Ma Rainey's Black Bottom' and 'Bo Weevil Blues.'

Ma Rainey was arrested in Chicago in 1925 when police responded to a noise complaint and found a room full of naked women in 'intimate;' situations. Rainey spent the night in jail for hosting an 'indecent party' and was bailed out the following morning by her friend and fellow blues singer Bessie Smith.

Ma Rainey continued performing for another seven years after her last recording in 1928. Quite often her audiences were racially segregated or exclusive. Her performance attire was extravagantly accessorised with sequins, diamonds and her trademark necklace made of gold coins. She performed with Louis Armstrong, Bessie Smith and Thomas Dorsey. Despite all of the trappings of fame, Rainey remained loyal to her southern, rural roots and to her audience. Rainey retired to her home town of Columbus after her mother and sister died in 1935. She managed two theatres that she had bought and became active in the Congregation of Friendship Baptist Church where her brother was a deacon. Ma Rainey died on 22 December 1939 from heart disease. The obituary in the local paper listed her as a housekeeper by profession.

Rainey was inducted into the Blues Foundation's Hall of Fame in 1983, and the Rock and Roll Hall of Fame in 1990 as an early influence. Ma Rainey, 'Mother of the Blues,' was honoured with a US postage stamp in 1994.

Bessie Smith (1894-1937)

The Greatest Blues Singer in History! Columbia Records released 44 of her recordings during her lifetime and sold 8 million units. She was born in Chattanooga, Tennessee, and was tall and striking - she wore wild costumes on stage. She starred in a film called *St Louis Blues* in 1929. She had bouts of alcoholic abuse but they never affected her performances. Bessie first married Earl Love who was from a prominent black Mississippi family. Love died soon after the wedding.

Her second marriage was to Jack Gee in 1923. Gee mismanaged her affairs so she never received any royalties and earned $125 per recording. Bessie's interest in women was first documented in 1926. Lillian Simpson was in the chorus of Bessie's show and she often slept in Bessie's room. Bessie kissed her in public and Lillian's objection was met with a swift rebuke: "The hell with you, bitch. I got twelve women on this show and I can have one every night if I want it."[59]

In 1929 Jack Gee went too far. He financed another singer's show with Bessie's money. Bessie was furious and hurt. She left Cincinnati and arrived by cab in Columbus, Ohio, at Gee's hotel where she proceeded to 'cut and dice' the treacherous husband. The marriage was over. In the summer of 1929, when Bessie's troupe played in Chicago, she rekindled her friendship with Richard Morgan, a bootlegger who was genuinely fond of Bessie. Morgan made Bessie happy and financially secure until she died in 1937.

Libby Holman (1904-1971)

Libby Holman was a Jewish American who invented the strapless gown and was a celebrated torch singer. (She introduced many classic torch songs including 'Body And Soul.') She appeared on Broadway and her New York town house was a centre for intellectual discussion and literary profile. She frequented Harlem and was a pillar of the entertainment society. She married the heir to the Reynolds tobacco fortune. When he was murdered she was arrested and later acquitted. The movie *Reckless* (1935) was based on her life story.[60]

Libby's bisexuality was famous and she partnered Josephine Baker, Tallulah Bankhead, Jane Bowles, Montgomery Clift, Gary Cooper, Jeanne Eagles, Lisabeth White Guthrie (her secretary), Luisa Carpenter du Pont-Jenny (the heiress who also had an affair with Tallulah's sister Eugenia) and Clifton Webb. [61]

Bisexuality was part of the club scene for audiences as well as performers, and many Harlem nightclubs catered to straights and gays together. Even though Libby Holman was married to a man, she visited Harlem, where she could not only act as a lesbian but even be outrageously gay touring nightspots with her lover Luisa Carpenter du Pont-Jenny dressed in identical men's suits and hats.

Josephine Baker (1906-1975)

Freda Josephine Carson was born in St Louis, Missouri, on 3 June 1906 to washerwoman Carrie McDonald and vaudeville drummer Eddie Carson. Josephine grew up cleaning houses and babysitting for wealthy white families. They were reported to have reminded her "be sure not to kiss the baby." She got a job as a waitress at The Old Chauffeur's Club when she was 13 years old.

While waiting tables she met and had a brief marriage to Willie Wells. Josephine never depended on a man for financial support , which was unusual for a woman of that era. Therefore, she never hesitated to leave when a relationship soured.

She was married and divorced three more times, to American Willie Baker in 1921 (whose last name she chose to keep), Frenchman Jean Lion in 1937 (from whom she attained French citizenship) and French orchestra leader Jo Bouillon in 1947.

Josephine Bake became a famous dancer in Paris. Her affairs included Ahmed ben Bachir (court chamberlain to the caliph of Spanish Morocco), George Balanchine (choreographer), Colette (author), Gaston Doumergue (president of France), Al Glaouni (the pasha of Marrakech), Duke Ellington (composer & musician), Gustav crown prince of Sweden, Ernest Hemingway (author), Libby Holman (singer), Benito Mussolini, Juan Peron (Argentinean dictator & husband of Evita), Pablo Picasso, Luigi Pirandello (Italian playwright), Max Reinhardt (director) and Clara Smith (singer).[62]

Josephine served France during World War Two; she performed for the troops, and was an honourable correspondent for the French Resistance (undercover work included smuggling secret messages written on her music sheets) and a sub lieutenant in the Women's Auxiliary Air Force. She was later awarded the Medal of the Resistance with Rosette and named a Chevalier of the Legion of Honour by the French government for hard work and dedication.

Josephine visited the United States during the 1950s and 1960s with renewed vigour to fight racism. When New York's popular Stork Club refused to serve her, she engaged in a media battle with pro-segregation columnist Walter Winchell. The National Association for the Advancement of Coloured People (NAACP) named May 20 Josephine Baker Day in honour of her efforts. She formed a family referred to as "The Rainbow Tribe." Josephine wanted to prove that "children of different ethnicities and religions could still be brothers."

During her visits to America, Josephine developed a close friendship with American artist Robert Brady and on a trip to Acapulco, Mexico, in September 1973 they exchanged marriage vows. On 8 April 1975, Josephine premiered at the Bobino Theatre in Paris. Celebrities such as Princess Grace of Monaco and Sophia Loren were in attendance. The reviews were among her best ever. Days later, however, Josephine slipped into a coma. She died from a cerebral haemorrhage at 5 a.m. on 12 April. More than 20,000 people crowded the streets of Paris to watch the funeral procession on its way to the Church of the Madeleine. The French government honoured her with a 21-gun salute, making Josephine Baker the first American woman buried in France with military honours. Her gravesite is in the Cimetière de Monaco, Monaco.

3. Film Personalities

The age of sexual enlightenment that flourished in pre-World War One Berlin spawned the first gay liberation movement led by Dr Magnum Hirschfield whose Institute for Sexual Science was the focal point of the battle against the anti-gay Paragraph 175 which outlawed homosexual acts between men. *Different From The Others* released in 1919, was a scare-tactic film to demonstrate that anybody who strayed from the established path of sex for procreation would die miserable and lonely. When the film was screened, these program notes were distributed to the audience: 'False beliefs... concerning a sector of male and female sexual behaviour known as homosexuality or love of the same sex have been predominant up to now and still influence large part of our population. These people are often regarded as wicked criminals and libertines. Scientific Research has determined that homosexuality is an inborn tendency for which the individual cannot be held responsible. In Germany, every thirtieth person has homosexual tendencies. Homosexuals are in every class, among the educated and the uneducated. The love for one's own sex can be just as pure and noble as love for the opposite sex, the only difference being the object of desire, not the nature of one's love.'

Films changed sexual awareness. They presented alternate methods to respond to situations. They provided material upon which to discuss many subjects that had not been included in conversation before that time. Movies were also an inexpensive courting and excursion destination.

'All great stars are bisexual in the performance mode. Dietrich herself once remarked, "Each man or woman should be able to find in the actress the thing he or she most desires and still be left with the promise that they will find something new and exciting every time they see her again." Her great skill lay in the personification of bisexuality as the performative sign of stardom."[63]

In 1997, Vito Russo's extraordinary book *The Celluloid Closet*, was adapted into a film by Rob Epstein and Jeffrey Friedman. In *Variety*, David Rooney writes: 'High on the list of lesbian icons is Marlene Dietrich in a man's suit in *Morocco* and Greta Garbo as Swedish bachelor-girl monarch *Queen Christina*. Moving into the 1950s, the documentary heralds the arrival of tough lesbians behind bars and the sleek socialite model, like Lauren Bacall in *Young Man With A Horn*, interpreted by screenwriter Jay Presson Allen as a warning for ladies to get back to the kitchen. Gay male characters became miserable or doomed, like Tom Lee's role in *Tea And Sympathy* and Sal Mineo's in *Rebel Without A Cause*. Man-to-man affinities come under scrutiny in films like *Spartacus*, with Tony Curtis wryly commenting on his deleted hot-tub scene with Laurence Olivier. Writer Gore Vidal discusses *Ben-Hur*, hilariously recounting his introduction of a gay frisson into the scenario with William Wyler's consent, but without actor Charlton Heston's knowledge.'

In 1969, in New York's Lower East Side, the police raided a gay bar called the Stonewall Inn. This was a routine raid. There was a dormant law on the city books of not serving alcohol to homosexuals. Around election time the police would make the rounds and harass and abuse the drag queens and homosexual or lesbian patrons. This time the "sissy boys" and the "tomboys" fought back and Gay Civil Rights was born in the United States.

Frank Bruni: "For the most part, the jaundiced eye cast on heterosexual characters is a phenomenon of independent film-making, and reflects both the rise of low-budget features and a simultaneous discovery of a rich market of gay and lesbian film-goers that is big enough and reliable enough to promise a return on relatively modest investments. Because these movies do not need to reach a diverse audience to succeed, their makers face no economic imperative to present fully-integrated, even-handed portraits of society. In fact, doing the opposite may be the more financially sound strategy. A celluloid world in which homosexuals are presented as the norm and heterosexuals as aberrations provides under-standable entertainment, not to mention a sense of overdue justice, for gay and lesbian movie-goers stepping into theatres from a society in which the opposite is often true."

He lists other gay-themed movies where heterosexual ridicule is an audience pleaser. *The Birdcage*, whose magic comes from the original stage show and French film *La Cage Aux Folles*, brings a whole new audience to this satisfying drama-comedy. In *To Wong Foo, Thanks For Everything, Julie Newmar*, one gay character says it best, "Sometimes it just takes a fairy" to effect communal change.

Frank Bruni: "These mainstream Hollywood movies do not go so far as to present homosexuality as an idealised norm. They make certain that for every moment a heterosexual in the audience feels a stab of recrimination there is another moment when he or she exorcises any discomfort with a good belly laugh at the limp-wristed man in a ridiculous dress."

For bisexuality or homosexuality there is no better goal than self-realisation, spiritually, socially, professionally, financially and sexually. The following profiles are the sexual characters that have influenced us with their art or their lives.

Anita Loos (1888-1981)

Loos' sexuality is undetermined but she lived and socialised with the main bisexual gang in Hollywood. Screenwriter, playwright and novelist, Anita was born in California and was a child actor. She was tiny, precocious and witty. Her talent was resourceful and endured. She was an immediate screenwriting success. Anita met Mary Pickford and wrote *The New York Hat* (1912). It was one of Pickford's last films for DW Griffith. This led to the Fairbanks connection where Anita concocted marvellous plots to sustain Fairbanks' dashing style of performance.

Anita married John Emerson, an actor, and wrote for silent pictures. In 1925 she wrote *Gentlemen Prefer Blondes*, made into a film in 1928 by Paramount starring Ruth Taylor as Lorelei. Anita Loos was friendly and familiar with many Hollywood luminaries including Greta Garbo, Tallulah Bankhead, George Cukor and Cecil Beaton. Cecil Beaton was her special friend and she helped him gain an introduction to Garbo. Anita was a terrific correspondent; in her newsy letter to Cecil during the love affair between Greta Garbo and Mercedes de Acosta, she wrote to Beaton: 'There has been so much going on in our set here that every time I think of writing I am swamped with the idea of trying to tell you it all. The Garbo-Mercedes business has been too amazing. They had terrible battles and Garbo left without saying goodbye. Then Mercedes flew to NY to see her and Garbo wouldn't. Mercedes flew back despondent, lost her job with MGM and is in the most awful state.'[64]

Her screenwriting continued with *The Struggle* (1931), *Red-Headed Woman* (1932), *Blondie Of The Follies* (1932), *San Francisco* (1936), *Saratoga* (1937), *The Women* (1939) and *Susan And God* (1940). Her last screenplay was the rewrite of *Gentlemen Prefer Blondes* in 1953. After a successful career screenwriting, Anita wrote authoritative books on Hollywood and liked to talk about the Golden Age and promote her books. She died in 1981 in New York. Her books include *A Girl Like I* (1966), *Kiss Hollywood Goodbye* (1974), *Cast Of Thousands* (1977) and *The Tamadge Girls* (1978).

Beatrice Lillie (1894-1989)

Beatrice Lillie was born Constance Sylvia Munston in Ontario, the daughter of a Canadian government official. She was an actress, singer and a popular comedienne of British and American revues and light plays. At 15 she left school to form a singing trio with her mother and her sister. She debuted in London in a 1914 revue and New York in 1924 with *Charlot's Revue*. Her friends included Noel Coward, Winston Churchill, George Bernard Shaw and Charlie Chaplin. She married Britain's Lord Peel and was widowed. In 1972 she wrote her autobiography, *Every Other Inch A Lady*.

Lillie's career began in films in 1926 with a comic masterpiece called *Exit Laughing*. No one was ever nastier in a nicer way than Lillie was. During her half-century theatrical career, Lillie earned the title 'the funniest woman in the world.' Hers was a sustained triumph of manic high spirits. The two most stylish lyricists wrote songs for her - Noel Coward wrote 'Marvellous Party' and Cole Porter wrote 'Mrs Lowsbrough - Goodbye.'

She hopped between the east and west coasts of America by train and between America and Europe by ship. Her posse included Gertrude Lawrence, Tallulah Bankhead and Adele Astaire, Fred's sister. Her female lovers included Le Gallienne, Judith Anderson and Katherine Cornell. She was still working in 1967 in *Thoroughly Modern Millie*.

Axel Madsen on Lillie: 'Lillie was ruthless, and unpredictable under any spotlight, and if her classic female clown can prove anything, it is that before the bold new world of end-of-the-century lesbian chic, there was more to women loving women than the "boring loyalty...earnestness... and complete lack of humour" that Cecil Beaton and Mercedes de Acosta made fun of. Like young Dietrich and Margo Lion doing *Sisters* on the 1920s Berlin stage, and k d lang singing her sultry ballads 1990s style, Lillie was always on the edge of the permissible.'[65]

Gertrude Lawrence (1898-1952)

The English actress and singer, Gertrude Lawrence was born Alexandre Dagmar Lawrence-Klasen. Performing on the musical stage from childhood, Lawrence made her New York debut (1924) in *Charlot's Revue* with Beatrice Lillie. A childhood friend of Noel Coward, she appeared with him in his *Private Lives* (1931) and *Tonight at 8:30* (1936). Her charm and magnetic personality in *Susan And God* (1937) and in such musicals as *Lady In The Dark* (1941) and *The King And I* (1951) endeared her to the public. In 1945 her autobiography *A Star Danced* was published. In 1950 she played Amanda in a film version of *The Glass Menagerie*. Popular songs were written for the successful performing partnership of Lillie and Lawrence.

Her lovers included Noel Coward, Beatrice Lillie and William Powell. She died in 1952.

Charles Laughton (1899-1962)

Laughton and Elsa Lanchester were British actors who married in 1929. They were happy for the first two years. An unpaid hustler finally alerted Elsa to Charles' love of boys. In reaction to this news, Elsa went deaf for a week as if her body muted what it didn't want to hear. They remained married for 33 years because public stigma would have destroyed Laughton's career were his sexuality to have become publicly known. Elsa demanded he remove the sofa where the lusty encounters occurred. They never had children but remained very close and loving. Meanwhile Charles continued looking for young trade and finally met two young men with whom relationships blossomed for 20 years or so. Elsa contented herself with taking discreet lovers and was a respected character actress.

Marlene Dietrich (1901-1992)

Marlene Dietrich was born Maria Magdalena Von Losch in Berlin. Her 1930 performance in *Blue Angel* (Josef Von Sternberg's film) catapulted her to international success. She established her sex goddess status with *Shanghai Express* and *Blond Venus* (1932). Marlene was married to Rudi Papilien, the father of her daughter, Maria. It was an open-ended marriage. He lived in Paris and they were loving and cordial in their relationship, as revealed through letters. But Marlene had to keep working to support her lifestyle and the employees that her lifestyle spawned.

'Marlene's lifestyle was as extravagant as Garbo's was miserly. Besides supporting the ocean front avenue menagerie, that is the rented villa, the staff, bodyguards and assorted hangers-on, her earnings kept Papilien in style in Paris and in transatlantic wanderings with Tami, and Marlene's mother in Berlin.'[66]

'Unlike the reclusive Garbo, Marlene was a shimmering and vibrant hedonist who frolicked in Hollywood night after night, sipping champagne with a trademark single white rose petal floating on the surface. Lesbians propositioned her in restaurant and nightclub restrooms. During World War Two, Dido Renoir, the Brazilian wife of director Jean Renoir, would remember Marlene asking her to come to the ladies' room with her. Dido assumed the reason was that the actress wanted to show off her famous legs, but Marlene told her she needed protection from the women who assailed her.'[67]

Lily Damita and Marlene Dietrich are reported to have become a rallying point for French exiles once the war began in France in June 1940.

'The war was Dietrich's Second Coming. She was not the only waning star to entertain the troops on endless USO tours, but better than old troopers such as Al Jolson, Noel Coward, Bob Hope and Maurice Chevalier, she remade her legend. Tirelessly and good-humouredly, she sang her movie songs, the international wartime ballad 'Lili Marlene,' and played a musical saw, a skill she had mastered for the Berlin stage, for half a million allied troops and war prisoners across North Africa and Europe. She had started right after Pearl Harbour and with Orson Welles performing for GIs passing through Los Angeles and emerged in 1945 with a one-woman show that gave her a worldwide audience she would draw on for the next thirty years.'[68]

During the 1950s, when older, exciting women's parts in film dried up, she had a successful cabaret career touring the world. Marlene had an affair with Mercedes de Acosta who was an author.

'Dietrich was noted for performing fellatio on her male lovers - it gave her the power to direct the scene - but preferred to go to bed with women. Women were better in bed, she said, "but you can't live with a woman."'[69]

Tallulah Bankhead (1902-1968)

Tallulah was born in 1902, the daughter of William Bankhead, the Speaker of the House, and Adelaide Eugenia Sledge. Her mother died shortly after Tallulah's birth. Tallulah adored her father. She never went too crazy if she felt it would hurt her father's government position. She often withdrew from her showbiz life to go on the campaign trail with him.

"My father warned me about men and booze, but he never mentioned a word about women and cocaine." Tallulah won a beauty contest and persuaded her father to let her move to New York. She worked as an actress. Her wit earned her membership to the Algonquin Club.[70] She went to London in 1923 with a show called *Dancers.* It ran for 344 performances. She basked in the admiration of London society who laughed at her jokes and admired her acting talent

"I don't know what I am, dahling. I've tried several varieties of sex. The conventional position makes me claustrophobic, and all the others give me either a stiff neck or lockjaw."

Amongst Tallulah's conquests were Gladys Bentley (a three-hundred pound black Mae West who composed and performed dirty songs... sometime in the 1920s, she put on a tuxedo and married a woman in a New Jersey civil ceremony), Marlon Brando, Yul Brynner, Winston Churchill, Katherine Cornell (actress), Laurette Taylor, Sybil Thorndyke, Douglas Fairbanks Junior (actor), Billie Holiday, Libby Holman, Beatrice Lillie, Hattie McDaniel and Burgess Meredith.[71]

In 1930, Tallulah signed with Paramount and starred in *Tarnished Lady* (1931) filmed in New York. George Cukor directed her and they remained lifelong friends from this meeting. Tallulah went to Hollywood for a year and rented the house of William Haines. (William Haines was the matinee idol fired by Louis B Mayer for refusing to live apart from his boyfriend.) Tallulah entertained and gave parties for Laurence Olivier and Jill Esmond (Laurence's lesbian wife), the Barrymores, Anita Loos and George Cukor and his gay crowd.

From 1933 to 1944 she was not making movies. To please her father she married John Emory, an actor, in 1937. When he died in 1941, she returned to her wild lifestyle. In 1939 *Little Foxes* opened in New York. She followed this success with Thornton Wilder's *The Skin Of Our Teeth* in 1942. *Girls About Town* was written by Zoe Akins for Tallulah and Lilyan Tashman.

Tallulah's films include: *My Sin* (1931), *The Cheat* (1931), *Lifeboat* (1944, directed by Alfred Hitchcock, this earned her the New York Screen Critics Award), *Main Street To Broadway* (1953) and *Die! Die! My Darling!* (1965).

Cary Grant (1904-1986)

Cary Grant was born Archibald Alexander Leach. At the age of 9, he lost his mother to a mental institute. Young Leach joined Bob Pender's troupe of knockabout comedians at the age of 14. He learned mime, acrobatics and picked up a cockney accent. When Archie was 16 the Troupe went to Broadway and they played 456 performances in New York. His stay in America lasted for two years and he returned to England where he had some success as a leading man on the stage.

By 1932 he was screen-tested in Hollywood by Paramount and debuted in *This Is The Night*: 'Movies from the 1930s through the 1950s used actors of this kind to illustrate a singular male beauty, witty and polished, uniting sensitivity of response to intense heterosexual glamour: Leslie Howard, Rex Harrison, Cary Grant, Fred Astaire, David Niven, Michael Wilding, George Hamilton. The idiomatic qualities are smoothness and elongation; smooth both in manner and appearance, long in ectomorphic height and Nordic cranial contour.'[72]

In *Blonde Venus* he was paired with Marlene Dietrich. In 1933, he co-starred with Mae West in *She Done Him Wrong*. It was a wildly successful comedy and they reprieved their duet in *I'm No Angel*. He epitomised the suave, debonair sophisticate. He starred with Katherine Hepburn in *The Philadelphia Story*. He also made *His Girl Friday*, *My Favourite Wife*, *Gunga Din*, *None But The Lonely Hearts*, *Arsenic And Old Lace*, *Suspicion*, *Notorious*, *To Catch A Thief* and *North By Northwest*. He played Cole Porter in the 1946 movie *Night And Day*.

Cary Grant married 4 times: Barbara Harris (and stayed with her until his death), Dyan Cannon (divorced in 1968), Betsy Drake (divorced 1962) and Barbara Hutton (divorced 1945). But Grant and Randolph Scott lived together in a gay relationship from 1933. He was also involved with Howard Hughes. All three men were married and bisexual![73] He donated all the profits from *The Philadelphia Story* and *Arsenic And Old Lace* to the British war effort. Cary Grant's death in 1986 was due to a major stroke prior to a performance of his one-man show *An Evening with Cary Grant*.

Joan Crawford (1904-1977)

Joan Crawford made over 80 films and survived in Hollywood for 40 years. In 1945 she won an Oscar for her performance in *Mildred Pierce*. Born Lucille LeSueur in San Antonio, Texas, her father deserted the family and from the age of twelve Lucille worked in boarding schools where the beatings were often and severe. At 20 she escaped to New York to become a dancer. On New Year's day 1925 she arrived in Los Angeles with a five-year contract at Paramount. She dieted and fixed her teeth. Before you knew it, Joan was a star.

Joan's marriage to Douglas Fairbanks Junior in 1929 was unpopular with his family to say the least. She aborted their child claiming it was a miscarriage and this resulted in their divorce. In 1933, Joan was involved with Clark Gable but although they remained friends until his death she said he wasn't much use in bed.

In October 1935, she married Franchot Tone, a wealthy Easterner. During this marriage she suffered 2 miscarriages and when she found Tone in bed with another woman she got rid of him in 1939. Now she focused on her children, determined to be a mother. She adopted 4 children and several biographies by these children have been published. Her ambition, rigorous schedule and stories of child abuse circulated amongst journalists. The publicity department of MGM quashed the rumours.

'Crawford was an earthy bisexual who went through men and, when they were available, young women, with the same ruthlessness she used to get to the top. Intimates called her Billie. More than one young woman reporter would tell of interviews at Crawford's home when the star, under the pretext of needing to change, invited the journalist to continue the conversation while she dressed for dinner. Once in the bedroom, Crawford made remarks about the colour co-ordination of the reporter's clothes and picking designer dresses from the closet, suggested the visitor slip out of her dress and try out several outfits. Christina Crawford, Joan's adopted daughter, would say that her mother tried to sleep with a hired nurse. "I knew about my mother's lesbian proclivities," Christina would write in *Mommie Dearest*, "and this only added to what I had figured out for myself.'"[74]

Joan was an opportunistic bisexual. One time she was introduced to Garbo at a dinner party. Crawford said of this meeting: "If ever there was a time in my life when I might have become a lesbian, that was it."[75]

She had already had an affair with director Dorothy Arzner. As a starving chorus girl in New York, Joan did 2 porn pictures: *Velvet Lips* and *The Casting Couch*. She and MGM attempted to buy up all the prints but they were not successful. Stills from the pictures have appeared in at least 2 books. She concluded her career serving on the board of Pepsi Cola thanks to her fourth husband.

According to Bette Davis: "She's slept with every male star in Hollywood except Lassie."

At her death of stomach cancer she was still in touch with 1,500 of her fans.

Greta Garbo (1905-1990)

Greta Garbo grew up in Stockholm as Greta Gustaffson, daughter of Karl and Anna. Karl died of alcoholism and tuberculosis at the age of 48. Greta and her father enjoyed reading stories out loud and they went to the theatre district together. After working in department stores and modelling hats she became one of only 6 accepted at the Dramaten, the official acting academy in Stockholm drama school. Her friend Mimi Pollock was accepted at the same time.

In 1923, aged 18, she was introduced to Mauritz Stiller. Stiller became her Svengali. He chose her stage name: Garbo. After *The Atonement Of Gosta Berling* was made in 1923, Garbo and Stiller were offered contracts by MGM in 1925. In the same year she made her first film in the United States, *The Torrent*, followed by *The Temptress* (1926), *Love* (1927), *A Woman Of Affairs* (1928). In 1930 she made her first talkie *Anna Christie*.

In 1929 Garbo's friend Salka Viertel,[76] who welcomed German exiles, invited Garbo to stop by and meet a new arrival, Mercedes de Acosta. Mercedes had heard that Garbo liked big clunky bracelets and so she gave her one and told her she had bought it for her in Berlin. 'The gesture sealed an intimate attachment that would last for decades. However different they, and a little later, Marlene Dietrich were, the longevity of these three women's love, rivalries, and on-and-off ardour and devotion can be seen as the overriding arch of Sapphic and bisexual love in Hollywood.'[77]

Stiller returned to Sweden and died there. After making 5 films, back-to-back, Garbo took a leave of absence and went home to Sweden. On board ship, she met the Count and Countess of Wachtmeister and had an affair with the countess, a tall vigorous woman 9 years older than her.

Garbo was nominated for an academy award for *Anna Christie*. *Mata Hari* followed in 1931. She starred opposite John Barrymore in *Grand Hotel* (1932) and was a great admirer of his acting. *Queen Christina* (1933) saw her reunited with John Gilbert. Her affection for him is memorialised in an erotic scene that succeeds without words. Their relationship off screen suffered due to Gilbert's alcoholism.

Then in 1935, MGM cast her as Anna Karenina. She outperformed herself. She plays a woman torn between two lovers and her son with depth and sensitivity. Clarence Brown, with whom she had a strong and understanding relationship, directed *Anna Karenina*. In 1939 she filmed *Ninotchka* with a comedic twist and her last film was *Two-Faced Woman*. In this film she worked with George Cukor, the gay director (previously she worked with him in *Camille*).

She left Hollywood and moved to New York where she lived until 84 years of age, dying in 1990. Garbo was romanced and obsessed over by a legion of fans, friends and committed lovers. They included Cecil Beaton (the British photographer), Louise Brook (actress), Fifi D'Orsay, Mercedes de Acosta (lesbian writer), Dolores Del Rio (actress), Marie Dressler, Paulette Duval, Gayelord Hauser (health guru), Maria Huxley (wife of Aldous Huxley), Joseph P Kennedy, Beatrice Lillie (actress), William S Paley (businessman and later head of CBS) and Salka Viertel (bisexual actress/writer).

Laurence Olivier (1907-1989)

Olivier is considered one of the finest actors of the twentieth century. He is reputed to have uttered Shakespeare's verse with an eloquence that caused English playwright Charles Bennett to characterise his delivery as if he were "actually thinking them." He began his career with the Birmingham Repertory Company, moved to London and joined the Old Vic Theatre, and became wildly popular for his interpretations of Shakespeare.

In modern drama he scored playing Archie Rice in John Osborne's *The Entertainer* (1957 and the 1960 film) and the father in Eugene O' Neill's play *Long Day's Journey Into Night* (1972).

Olivier married three times. His first wife was Jill Esmond. 'Their marriage was a sham. On the wedding night she turned away from her husband in revulsion. The two had appeared in the Broadway production of Noel Coward's *Private Lives* and were now in Hollywood where RKO had signed them to a forty-week contract.'[78]

Olivier was tormented with sexual guilt and conflict but that did not stop him having a wonderful time doing fine work and consorting with Hollywood's wildest and brightest, among them Tallulah Bankhead.

His next wife was Vivien Leigh. Vivien had fallen in love with him years before when they performed together in *Hamlet* at Kronberg Castle, Elsinore, in 1937. They made 3 movies together: *Fire Over England* (1937), *21 Days Together* (1940) and *That Hamilton Woman* (1941). They were married for two decades and performed in films and on stage together throughout the world. Vivien had her mentally unstable moments when she would cruise around town looking for trade to satisfy her manic-depressive nymphomaniac tendencies.

Laurence Olivier was knighted in 1947 and made a life peer in 1970. He had affairs with Noel Coward (1930-1933) and Danny Kaye. According to David Spoto: '...for by this time Olivier and Danny Kaye were lovers... At first Vivien had merely thought Kaye rude arriving at their house unannounced at odd hours, without invitation or permission but Olivier was also spending long, late hours with him and the affair - at first rampant gossip and then a widespread belief in Hollywood, New York and the Caribbean (where the relationship continued irregularly for several years) - was no secret to Vivien nor did Olivier deny it.'[79]

Then Laurence married actress/director Joan Plowright. From 1962-1973, he was director of the National Theatre Company. In 1984 his autobiography, *Confessions Of An Actor*, was published and he was awarded The Order of Merit. During the shoot of *Marathon Man*, upon learning that his co-star Dustin Hoffman had stayed up for two days to look suitably exhausted he remarked: "You should try acting, my boy it's much easier." Olivier's motion pictures include *Wuthering Heights* (1939), *Rebecca* (1939), *Pride And Prejudice* (1940), *Henry V* (1945), *Hamlet* (1948) and *Richard III* (1955).

Errol Flynn (1909-1959)

Errol Flynn was born in Hobart, Tasmania, of American-Irish heritage. He ran away from home all the time and after secondary school travelled the South Seas. He was six foot two inches tall. He married three times, to: Lily Damita (a bisexual), Patrice Wymore and Norah Eddington.

Flynn was never faithful. He enjoyed going to Mexico and catching the live sex shows. On at least two occasions he was charged with rape and, though acquitted, his guilt was never totally absolved. Errol Flynn was one of cinema's greatest swashbuckling actors in the 1930s and 1940s. He was Captain Blood and Robin Hood. Flynn was signed by Warner Brothers and played larger than life heroes for the next 15 years.

In the 1950s he moved first to Europe and then to Jamaica and died at 50 of a heart attack due to late nights, alcohol and narcotics. After his death Charles Higham published a biography which claimed that the swashbuckling actor had aided the Nazis and the Japanese causes during World War Two and that he was bisexual. The book stated that Flynn had two homosexual affairs: one with Tyrone Power and the other with the writer Truman Capote.

Danny Kaye (1913 -1987)

Danny Kaye was a comic actor. Born in New York City, he dropped out of school at age 13. His career began as a comic in the 'Borscht Circuit' of the Catskills, then he worked as a singer and dancer in nightclubs and vaudeville until he made his Broadway debut in 1939 in the *Straw Hat Revue*. In 1940, *Lady In The Dark* was a musical success and drew the attention of critics and agents.

In 1940 he married Sylvia Fine, a songwriter who managed his career. His genius was for mimicry, controlled slapstick and spoken song delivery. He appeared in a series of successful films from *Up In Arms* (1944) through *The Court Jester* (1956), all concocted primarily as vehicles for his versatility. During the 1950s Danny Kaye and Laurence Olivier were involved. There are funny stories of Danny Kaye dressing up as a customs official supposedly to amuse and surprise Laurence Olivier.

'Danny Kaye has a big fan in Michael Bronski who is delivering a video and lecture presentation at Harvard Yard, London on the sexuality of Danny Kaye. In response to questions about Kaye's sexuality Bronski displays acumen and intuition in evaluating the gay, flighty, queeny escapist individual who inhabited the lead roles of Danny Kaye's films. He was a positive view of effeminate behaviour before it was politically correct to recognise that being deviant in any way was not necessarily a bad thing. The confessional nature of labelling and the cross-hanging attitude of pantywaists imply that everyone and everything has been suppressed for ever and we know in our personal experience that that is not true! Here's Bronski: "Is Danny Kaye part of gay history? Of course he is, whether he slept with men or not (and I think there is more than enough evidence to suggest that he did). Kaye looks and sounds like a queen. At a very critical and conservative time in US history and culture he gave us this very flamboyant style and performances that made it all right, to some degree, to be not traditionally masculine. And his movies are great - funny, silly and almost always moving."'[80]

Tyrone Power (1914-1958)

Tyrone Power was born in 1914 to a family of actors that could be traced to the eighteenth century. His great-grandfather was a famed Irish comedian. His father was a huge star in the theatre and later in films. His mother, Patia Power, was an actress and drama coach. Ty was a sickly child. When his parents divorced his mother took him and his sister Anne to the East Coast but he corresponded regularly with his father and was inspired to pursue acting due to his father's interest and support. He worked with his father for a season in Chicago and held his father in his arms when he died of a heart attack. In 1936, a screen test led to a contract with 20th Century-Fox. During World War Two he served in the Marine Corps. After the war, he returned to Hollywood and continued to act in films.

'After Fay Wray found Tyrone Power too fond of the boys, Brand covered Ty's exuberant homosexuality with well-publicised dates with Fox contract players Loretta Young, Janet Gaynor, and Sonja Henie. When Power became world-famous and under greater scrutiny, Brand publicised the star's secret romance with newcomer Annabella, a French actress of androgynous manners who had starred in René Clair's *Le Million*.'[81]

In 1939 he married Annabella and remained married to her until 1948. In 1949 he married Linda Christian, and they had a daughter together, Taryn.

Charles Higham's biography *Howard Hughes: The Secret Life* says, 'Hughes became bisexual, and was later to have affairs with several male stars, including Cary Grant and Tyrone Power.'

Gore Vidal (1925-)

Gore Vidal was born in West Point, New York and his first novel *Williwaw* achieved success in 1946.

Quotes from Gore Vidal:

"A narcissist is someone better looking than you are."

"Most lives are spent putting on and taking off masks."

"The only absolute attainment is absolute abandonment."

"Sex is. There is nothing more to be done about it. Sex builds no roads, writes no novels, and sex certainly gives no meaning to anything in life but itself."

"I'm in favour of any form of sexual relationship that gives pleasure to those involved. And I have never heard a convincing argument to the contrary."

"I never miss a chance to have sex or appear on television."

James Dean (1931-1955)

James Dean died at the age of 24 and his premature death immortalised him. Andy Warhol said he was "the damaged but beautiful soul of our time" whereas Humphrey Bogart said, "Dean died at just the right time. He left behind a legend. If he had lived he would never have been able to live up to his publicity."[82]

His friends included Eartha Kitt and Judy Collins. His big love affair was with Pier Angeli whose mother couldn't stand James Dean. Pier decided to marry Vic Damone and 2 days later Dean was dead. A cult grew around him and whether he was gay, straight or bisexual. Obviously he was bisexual as he was kept for a while by Rogers Brackett, a Hollywood producer and admitted to having had at least 5 studio executives service him. He commented, "I've had my cock sucked by five of the big names in Hollywood, and I think it's pretty funny because I wanted more than any thing to get some little part, something to do and they'd invite me for fancy dinners..." About being gay he said, "Well, I'm certainly not going to go through life with one hand tied behind my back."[83]

"I kissed the medic," was his remark when asked about how he had avoided the draft.

4. Films

For many years within the entertainment industry African Americans, Hispanics, homosexuals and bisexuals were cast as criminals and deceitful people both in bed and in life. In *The Celluloid Closet*, Vito Russo addressed the poor characterisation of gays and bisexuals in the movies up until the 1980s. Bisexuals in particular were cast as vicious killers and immoral renegades, the assumption being that they were bisexual and therefore not normal and it followed therefore psychotic.

Independent film production and a rash of young, clear-thinking writers shook up the stereotypes. They revitalised the casting of films and television with heroes and villains of every type. Network television and film studios were quick to catch on to the profitable bandwagon. Storylines including gay-friendly material made their way into sitcoms causing Jesse Helms and Dr Laura to have apoplectic fits. Entertainment marketing departments explained this to their executive branch: why appeal to one homogenous group when you can access the gay subculture? Include all types and develop a new majority.

The neglected minority became a strong consumer force. When grouped together they represent a new sales demographic.

Films often rewrite history and they are adept at covering up or demonising the sexuality of the hero. *The Agony And The Ecstasy* (1965) and *Khartoum* (1966), for example, implied that it was better to live a tortured life than own up to the fact that one was homosexual or bisexual. It took the AIDS epidemic for people to gather together and rise above prejudice to display compassion.

The following chronological lists of films can be used as a rough indication of how attitudes to bisexual characters have changed, or not, over the decades.

Films With Bisexual Heroes Or Villains

Mädchen In Uniform 1931. Starring Hertha Thiele.

The Children's Hour 1962. Audrey Hepburn and Shirley MacLaine are accused of having "sinful knowledge of one another."

The Balcony 1963. Shelley Winters as a madam who has a thing for her bookkeeper (Lee Grant).

Bonnie And Clyde 1967. Clyde's sexuality changed for the screen from bisexual to impotent.

The Fox 1968. Starring Sandy Dennis, Keir Dullea, Anne Heywood.

Barbarella 1968. Anita Pallenberg as the Black Queen and John Philip Law as a gay angel.

The Prime Of Miss Jean Brodie 1969. Starring Maggie Smith, Robert Stephens, Jane Carr.

The Christine Jorgensen Story 1970. John Hansen acts out the famous sex change story.

Sunday, Bloody Sunday 1971. Starring Peter Finch, Glenda Jackson, Murray Head.

Cabaret 1972. Michael York as bisexual Brian.

The Day Of The Jackal 1973. Edward Fox kills a gay man he meets in a bathhouse.

The Rocky Horror Picture Show 1976. Barry Bostwick, Susan Sarandon, Tim Curry.

Alexandria...Why? 1978. Autobiographical film featuring a love affair between an aristocratic nationalist and a young English soldier.

By Design 1981. Lesbian fashion designers contrive to have a baby by looking for a substitute father.

The Color Purple 1985. The love and intimacy between Whoopi Goldberg & Margaret Shug is indicated but their love scene was not included.

Apartment Zero 1988. Starring Hart Bochner, Colin Firth, Dora Bryan, James Telfer.

My Own Private Idaho 1990. Starring Keanu Reeves and River Phoenix as hustlers travelling to Idaho on a journey of self-discovery.

Henry & June 1990. Starring Richard E Grant, Maria de Medeiros, Fred Ward. Anaïs Nin, Henry and June Miller in a love quadrangle in 1930s Paris.

The Flavor Of Corn 1991. The story of Lorenzo's trials and tribulations with women and the comfort of his friend Dulio.

The Crying Game 1992. An IRA adventure where things are not what they seem.

The Wedding Banquet 1993. Starring Mitchell Lichtenstein, Winston Chao, May Chin.

Orlando 1993. Based on the novel by Virginia Woolf.

Threesome 1994. Starring Lara Flynn Boyle, Josh Charles, Stephen Baldwin.

Carrington 1995. Chronicles the affair of Dora Carrington (painter) and Lytton Strachey (biographer who was part of the Bloomsbury set).

Bound 1995. Classic Film Noir gay/lesbian suspense movie starring Jennifer Tilly and Gina Gershon.

Dry Cleaning 1997. A couple who owns a dry-cleaning establishment meets a couple who cross-dress and soon they are invited to visit their house...

The Opposite Of Sex 1998. A 16-year-old visits her half-brother who is gay. She ends up seducing his boyfriend, wreaking havoc in all their lives.

Trick 1999. Starring Tori Spelling, Christian Campbell.

Wonderland 1999. Lonely Londoners looking for love.

Just One Time 1999. Starring Lane Janger, Joelle Carter, Jennifer Esposito.

But I'm A Cheerleader 2000. Comedy about gay and bisexual teens committed to an institution that attempts to deprogram them sexually.

East Of A 2000. Starring Patrick Breen, Glen Chin, David Alan Grier, Rashida Jones.

Next Best Thing 2000. Surprise pregnancy complicated by parents being best friends and dad being gay.

Anders Als Die Anderen 1919. Pioneer gay German liberation film.

Bumping Into Broadway 1919. Gus Leonard in drag as the landlady of a theatrical boarding house.

Ben-Hur 1926. An erotic scene of a naked slave chained to the galley wall.

The Broadway Melody 1929. A gay costume designer.

Blood Money 1933. Sandra Shaw in a tuxedo.

Camille 1937. Rex O'Malley as Garbo's gay friend.

Dangerously They Live 1942. Connie Gilchrist as a Nazi lesbian.

Chu Hai Tang 1943. A general and a female impersonator from the Peking opera.

Un Chant d'Amour 1947. A revolutionary film about homoeroticism and repression.

Crossfire 1947. A story about homophobia changed to one about anti-Semitism.

The Damned (*Les Maudits*) 1947. Michel Auclair plays a homosexual.

Caged 1950. Lesbianism in a woman's prison.

Cinderella 1950. Jock and Gus-Gus aren't just good friends.

Cat On A Hot Tin Roof 1958. Why couldn't Paul Newman sleep with Elizabeth Taylor? A mystery movie.

Ben-Hur 1959. Submerged gay subtext between Messala and Ben-Hur.

Billy Budd 1962. Terence Stamp drives the sailors crazy.

The Best Man 1964. Cliff Robertson as the presidential candidate accused of homosexuality.

Darling 1965. Julie Christie has a gay photographer friend, and a bisexual waiter sleeps with them both.

The Chelsea Girls 1966. Faggots and dykes with messy apartments and boring opinions.

Midnight Cowboy 1969. Tilting at skyscrapers, a naive male prostitute and his sickly friend struggle to survive on the streets of New York.

The Damned 1969. Helmut Berger does Dietrich; the night of the long knives as an underwear party.

The Conformist 1970. If you sleep with your family chauffeur as a child it'll make you a fascist.

Myra Beckinridge 1970. Starring John Huston, Raquel Welch, Genevieve Waite, Rex Reed, Farrah Fawcett.

Death In Venice 1971. Dirk Bogarde as Ascenbach. Brooding slow study of one last love as Ascenbach waits to die in the loveliness of Venice.

Day For Night 1973. Jean-Pierre Aumont is given a handsome young lover but loses him in a car crash.

Army Of Lovers or *Revolt Of The Perverts* 1978. A view of the American Gay Movement

BOOM! 1968. Noel Coward as the Witch of Capri.

La Cage Aux Folles 1978. The first gay box-office smash.

The 4th Man 1984. Directed by Paul Verhoeven.

Before Stonewall 1985. Documentary history of pre-Stonewall gay liberation movement with rare film footage.

Caravaggio 1986. A highly personal, idiosyncratic meditation on the painter through his life and work.

The Celluloid Closet 1995. With Susie Bright, Lily Tomlin, Quentin Crisp, Tony Curtis.

To Wong Fu, Thanks For Everything, Julie Newmar 1995. Three drag queens break down in a small town and transform the town and everyone who lives there.

Gay Themed Films

Adam's Rib 1949. David Wayne "wouldn't have far to go" to be a woman.

The Big Sky 1952. Howard Hawks, Kirk Douglas and Dewey Martin rough it.

Advise And Consent 1962. Don Murray as Brig Anderson, the senator with a secret.

Becket 1964. A gay love story.

Bus Riley's Back In Town 1965. Harvey Hart as a lecherous gay mortician.

Belle De Jour 1967. Genevieve Page as a lesbian madam.

The Boys In The Band 1970. The first Hollywood film in which all the principal characters are homosexual.

Pink Flamingoes 1973. John Waters' all-American tale of competition and status, starring Divine.

Busting 1974. Sleazy gay bars, tearoom cruisers and hustlers versus the vice squad.

California Split 1974. A lesbian waitress doesn't fall for Elliot Gould or George Segal so they belittle a transvestite.

The Day Of The Locust 1975. Stars former homosexual John Atherton and features Paul Jabara as an art deco transvestite.

The Best Way (*La Meilleure Façon de Marcher*) 1976. Tea and Sympathy with a French accent and guts.

Casanova 1976. He tried men too!

The Choirboys 1977. Homophobic cops, and fags with pink poodles.

The Consequence 1977. Two gay lovers betrayed by the world around them.

California Suite 1978. Michael Caine as the gay husband of movie star Maggie Smith.

La Cage Aux Folles II 1980. Dimwit sequel featuring Albin jumping out of a cake looking like Ethel Merman.

Cruising 1980. A policeman discovers his own homosexuality and becomes a killer.

Chanel Solitaire 1981. Frivolous romantic nonsense about Coco Chanel including a brief reference to her lesbian affair with Misia Sert.

The Clinic 1982. Australian farce set in a VD clinic with several gay characters sprinkled throughout.

Another Country 1984 Sumptuously romanticised version of the Guy Burgess story, linking homosexuality with politics in a very tenuous manner.

La Cage Aux Folles III 1985. Hideously boring crap that took five screenwriters to put together.

Desert Hearts 1985. From Jane Rule's 1964 book. The lesbian love story of a casino worker and a professor.

A Chorus Line 1985. Timid bowdlerisation of the original musical with gay monologue cut to ribbons for a teen audience.

After Hours 1985. Mark, a lonely homosexual, is picked up by Griffin Dunne.

Buddies 1985. The first narrative feature about the AIDS crisis is personal and shattering. A story of love and politics.

Colonel Redl 1985. Head of Austrian imperial secret service exposed as homosexual and spy.

Blue Velvet 1986. Dean Stockwell can easily be read as gay if you buy the idea that David Lynch is recreating the 1950s here.

The Boys Next Door 1986. Fascinating violent splatter film about psychologically disturbed homosexual.

The Living End 1991. Two fatalistic LA boys - one's an impulsive, on-the-edge psycho cutie; the other listens to The Smiths a lot, and likes Godard movies - discover they're HIV positive and set about on an unplanned, unhinged serio-comic spree of violence and abandon.

Salmonberries 1991. k d lang as a butch Alaskan pipeline worker demonstrates the heightened anguish of squelched desire for a female librarian.

And The Band Played On 1993. The story of the discovery and investigation of AIDS.

The Adventure of Priscilla Queen of the Desert 1994. Starring Terence Stamp.

Go Fish 1994. A romantic comedy that follows the lives of a group of lesbians.

Eclipse 1994. Mathew Ferguson videos the goings-on in Toronto of ten people during an eclipse

Jeffrey 1995. A faithful adaptation of the mega-hit off-Broadway play. The story of a sexually compulsive gay man who one day, because of AIDS, refuses to ever copulate again. "Sex was never meant to be safe, negotiated or fatal."

French Twist 1995. A very funny film about Marijo who falls for Loli, Laurent's wife. They fight over her.

Incredibly True Adventures Of Two Girls In Love 1995. Lesbian love story written and directed by Maria Maggenti starring Laura Halloman and Nicole Parker.

Beautiful Thing 1995. Compassionate gay love story set in a British housing project.

When Night Is Falling 1995. A French woman who is engaged realises that she is a lesbian.

Everything Relative 1996. A group of lesbian and straight women who went to school together in the late 1970s are reunited when one of them has a baby.

Late Bloomers 1996. Carly, a housewife with two kids, falls in love with Dinah the geometry teacher and basketball coach.

The Watermelon Woman 1996. A documentary about 'Fae Richards,' an actress who played African American parts in early movies and had an affair with a white woman.

The Johns 1996. Considered an impartial assessment of hustler life.

Different For Girls 1997. This is the best film. I saw it and watched it three times I was so enchanted.

Ma Vie En Rose 1997. Story of Ludovic, a little girl born in a boy's body. The film is full of childhood magic contrasting with its controversial subject.

Kiss Me Guido 1997. An actor wants to move to Manhattan.

High Art 1997. An innovative photographic magazine employs Syd whose neighbour is such a photographer. The neighbour Lucy and her German girlfriend are druggies; one thing leads to another...

Billy's Hollywood Screen Kiss 1998. Written and directed by Tommy O'Haver from his short film Catalina, starring Sean P Hayes as Billy and Brad Rowe as Gabriel.

Three To Tango 1999. Confusion and intentions motivate this spry comedy.

If These Walls Could Talk 2 2000. Ellen DeGeneres shows us three lifetimes of lesbians in America.

Sexually Exploitative Films

Blood And Roses 1960. Roger Vadim lesbian vampires strike again.

The Anniversary 1966. Bette Davis' transvestite son steals women's nylons from clothes lines.

Bedazzled 1967. Two of the seven deadly sins, vanity and envy, are gay stereotypes.

Caprice 1967. Ray Walston as a transvestite killer.

Les Biches 1968. A lesbian zipless fuck.

Beyond The Valley Of The Dolls 1970. Middlebrow trash with a homophobic attitude.

The Boston Strangler 1968. Hurd Hatfield as a gay murder suspect.

The Gay Deceivers 1969. Two straight all-American boys play sissy to dodge the draft; they move into a swishy all-gay LA apartment complex, and a comedy of misunderstanding ensues. It's lurid, weird and unintentionally funny.

Bloody Mama 1970. Dominant, aggressive mother; absent father.

The Anderson Tapes 1971. Martin Balsam as a cowardly gay thief.

Caged Heat 1972. Lesbian sub-plot.

Cleopatra Jones 1973. Shelley Winters as Mommy, a lesbian gang leader.

Butley 1974. Gay teacher Alan Bates makes everybody miserable.

Barry Lyndon 1975. A gratuitous and offensive scene shows two gay soldiers bathing in a river.

Cleopatra Jones And The Casino Of Gold 1975. Stella Stevens as a lesbian dragon-lady dope seller.

Car Wash 1976. Antonio Fargas as the militant faggot transvestite.

The Betsy 1978. Paul Rudd as a gay who commits suicide.

Blood Brothers 1978. A gay jeweller hates his father.

American Gigolo 1980. A gay killer, a lesbian pimp and a gay wife beater.

Come Back To The Five And Dime, Jimmy Dean, Jimmy Dean 1983. Karen Black as the transsexual who comes back to haunt her childhood friends.

Angel 1984. According to the *New York Times*, 'one of the top sleeze-mobiles of 1984.' Includes a tacky drag queen.

Beverly Hills Cop 1984. Eddie Murphy's mindless fag routine is violently homophobic.

Basic Instinct 1992. GLAAD staged a number of protests as a result of the bias against gays and bisexuals shown in this cacophony of false information and misleading behavioural conclusions.

Notes

1. *Hijras: Who We Are* by Meena Balaji and other eunuchs.
2. E-mail from Nathan: 'Dear Angela, Thank you for your articles. I agree that there is much gender panic. However being transsexual myself, it seems it's always straight, gay or bi. I know it's confusing to a lot of people but gender is one thing and orientation is another. I believe two-spirited refers to people born in the wrong body. I wear my flesh but I do not see with it. It's sad but people do not know there are choices. Many do not have the courage but do have the knowledge. Even with my own situation I feel alone. If I venture to read a book on the subject, it is written by some not so healthy people. Sexes and genders are segregated just the way blacks and whites used to be (and still are). Please WRITE A BOOK!!!! Would like to hear your thoughts on this subject. You're beautiful. Just keep on being you.'

   Angela's e-mail to Nathan: 'I am writing a book, but in the meantime, my buddy, Jayne County has written a brilliant book, *Man Enough To Be A Woman*. I am sure you have already read it but if you haven't; please do! You will laugh, she is the best and funniest writer.'

3. http://www.ilga.org/Information/asi..._eunuch_pioneers_in_indian_poli.htm
4. *Sex In History* by Reay Tannahill, page 179.
5. Al-Mu'izz's instructor in the art of writing was a Saqlabi eunuch. Another Saqlabi was his sahib al-sitr (the bearer of the veil behind which the ruler spoke to the people), who carried out delicate diplomatic missions to the chiefs of the Kutama Berbers. Al-'Aziz kept about 10,000 slave girls and eunuchs. In terms of wealth and power, the eunuch Barjawan was typical of the top echelon of the ruling circles. A quarter in Cairo was named after him - his residence is reputed to have been there. Barjawan had large stables and his inheritance included a great quantity of textiles, many books and some 30,000 dinars in cash. None of the other eunuchs in Fatimid Egypt reached the same pinnacle of power as Barjawan. (http://www.fordham.edu/halsall/med/lev.html)
6. *Sex In History* by Reay Tannahill, pages 252-253.

7. *The Berdache Spirit* by Wendy Susan Parker. http://www.nu-woman.com/berdache.htm

8. Davis' book benefits from her scholarly experience as librarian in Sarasota for many years.

9. *The First Sex* by Elizabeth Gould Davis, pages 33-34.

10. *The First Sex* by Elizabeth Gould Davis, pages 34-35. She continues: 'The first males were mutants, freaks produced by some damage to the genes caused perhaps by disease or a radiation bombardment from the sun. Maleness remains a recessive genetic trait like colour-blindness and haemophilia with which it is linked. The suspicion that maleness is abnormal and that the Y chromosome is an accidental mutation boding no good for the race is strongly supported by the recent discovery by geneticists that congenital killers and criminals are possessed of not one but two Y chromosomes, bearing a double dose, as it were, of genetically undesirable maleness. If the Y chromosome is a degeneration and a deformity of the female X chromosome, then the male sex represents a degeneration and deformity of the female.'

11. Dr Fritz Klein's *The Bisexual Option* (1993) was written by a therapist and introduced The Klein Sexual Orientation Scale with seven variables: sexual attraction; sexual behaviour; sexual fantasies; emotional preference; social preference; heterosexual or homosexual lifestyle; and self-identification.

12. *The Bisexual Option* by Dr Fritz Klein, page 15.

13. *The Bisexual Option* by Dr Fritz Klein, page 27.

14. *The Bisexual Option* by Dr Fritz Klein, page 169.

15. *The Rock 'n' Roll Almanac* by Mark Bego 1996.

16. *The Use Of Pleasure* by Michel Foucault, Volume 2 page 188.

17. *Sexual Personae* by Camille Paglia, page 100.

18. *Sex In History* by Reay Tannahill, page 84.

19. *Sex In History* by Reay Tannahill, page 85.

20. In 1640 the Dutch military attaché visited her court and observed that she dressed as a man and had a harem of young men who dressed as women and attended her. Other early reports from Angola make it clear that Nzinga's behaviour was not some personal idiosyncrasy, but based on beliefs that recognised gender as

situational and symbolic as much as a personal innate characteristic of the individual. A result of these beliefs was the presence of an alternative gender role among the tribes of the Kongo and Ndonga kingdoms. According to Andrew Battel, an English prisoner of the Portuguese in the 1580s, natives of the Dombe area were "beastly in their living, for they have men in women's apparel, whom they keep among the wives."

21. LesbianPoetry@sappho.com Biographical writing copyright © 1995 Alexandria North

22. *Sex In History* by Reay Tannahill, page 87.

23. *Sexual Personae* by Camille Paglia.

24. *The Bisexual Option* by Dr Fritz Klein.

25. *Sexual Personae* by Camille Paglia, page 134.

26. *Sexual Personae* by Camille Paglia, page 138.

27. http://www.fordham.edu/halsall/pwh/hoveden1.html

28. *Artist and Aristocrat: A Biography of Michelangelo: The Complete Sculpture, Painting, Architecture*

29. *Sexual Personae* by Camille Paglia, page 198.

30. *Sexual Personae* by Camille Paglia, page 200.

31. *The Intimate Sex Lives Of Famous People* by Irving, Amy, Sylvia Wallace & David Wallechinsky, pages 443-444.

32. *The Intimate Sex Lives Of Famous People* by Irving, Amy, Sylvia Wallace & David Wallechinsky, page 443.

33. *The Secret Sex Lives Of Famous People* by Irving, Amy, Sylvia Wallace & David Wallechinsky, page 455.

34. Casanova has chapters on his visits with Voltaire and the wide range of subjects they discussed. Their conversations centred on the accomplishments or lack thereof of mutual friends and enemies. I tried to find a discussion on sex included in Casanova's narrative of their meetings but I found none.

35. *Sexual Personae* by Camille Paglia, page 144.

36. *The Secret Sex Lives Of Famous People* by Irving, Sylvia, Amy Wallace & David Wallechinsky, page 40.

37. *The Secret Sex Lives Of Famous People* by Irving, Sylvia, Amy Wallace & David Wallechinsky, page 392.

38. *The Intimate Sex Lives Of Famous People* by Irving, Amy, Sylvia Wallace & David Wallechinsky, pages 485-488.

39. *The Intimate Sex Lives Of Famous People* by Irving, Amy, Sylvia Wallace & David Wallechinsky, page 102.

40. *The Bisexual Option* by Dr Fritz Klein, page 140.

41. *Vice Versa: Bisexuality And The Eroticism Of Everyday Life* by Marjorie Garber, page 185.

42. *Vice Versa: Bisexuality And The Eroticism Of Everyday Life* by Marjorie Garber, page 177.

43. *The Intimate Sex Lives Of Famous People* by Irving Wallace, Amy Wallace and Sylvia Wallace & David Wallechinsky, page 426.

44. *The Secret Sex Lives Of Famous People* by Irving, Amy, Sylvia Wallace & David Wallechinsky, page 154.

45. *The Intimate Sex Lives Of Famous People* by Irving, Amy, Sylvia Wallace & David Wallechinsky, pages 138-140.

46. *The Sewing Circle* by Axel Madsen, page 152.

47. *The Bisexual Option* by Dr Fritz Klein, page 147.

48. *The Bisexual Option* by Dr Fritz Klein, pages 147-149.

49. *Vice Versa: Bisexuality And The Eroticism Of Everyday Life* by Marjorie Garber, page 106.

50. *The Intimate Sex Lives Of Famous People* by Irving, Amy, Sylvia Wallace & David Wallechinsky, page 187.

51. *The Sewing Circle* by Axel Madsen, page 152.

52. *The Sewing Circle* by Axel Madsen, page 152.

53. *Vice Versa: Bisexuality And The Eroticism Of Everyday Life* by Marjorie Garber, page 76.

54. *Vice Versa: Bisexuality And The Eroticism Of Everyday Life* by Marjorie Garber, page 77.

55. *Vice Versa: Bisexuality And The Eroticism Of Everyday Life* by Marjorie Garber, page 78.

56. www.kirjasto.sci.fi/dbarnes.htm

57. *Vice Versa: Bisexuality And The Eroticism Of Everyday Life* by Marjorie Garber, page 51.

58. Deirdre Bair interviewed in www.salon.com

59. *The Intimate Sex Lives Of Famous People* by Irving, Amy, Sylvia Wallace & David Wallechinsky, page 239.

60. *Dreams That Money Can Buy: The Tragic Life Of Libby Holman* by Jon Bradshaw is her most recent biography.

61. *Did She Or Didn't She?* by Mart Martin, page 83.

62. *Did She Or Didn't She?* by Mart Martin, page 9.

63. *Vice Versa: Bisexuality And The Eroticism Of Everyday Life* by Marjorie Garber, page 140

64. *Vickers Loving Garbo*, Anita Loos' 29 September 1932 letter to Cecil Beaton, page 4.

65. *The Sewing Circle* by Axel Madsen, page 122.

66. *The Sewing Circle* by Axel Madsen, page 76.

67. *The Sewing Circle* by Axel Madsen, page 70.

68. *The Sewing Circle* by Axel Madsen, page 189.

69. *The Sewing Circle* by Axel Madsen, page 71.

70. The Algonquin Round table was an informal gathering at the Algonquin hotel for lunch. The meetings began in 1919 and continued until 1943. The players were Dorothy Parker, Alexander Woolcott, Heywood Broun, Robert Benchly, Robert Sherwood, George S Kaufman, Franklin P Adams, Marc Connelly, Harold Ross, Harpo Marx and Russell Crouse. The group was known for lively and witty conversation. http://oakshire.ionestudios.com/%7Eneil/algonq.html

71. *Did She Or Didn't She?* by Mart Martin, page 11.

72. *Sexual Personae* by Camille Paglia, page 533.

73. *Vice Versa: Bisexuality And The Eroticism Of Everyday Life* by Marjorie Garber, page 147.

74. *The Sewing Circle* by Alex Madsen, page 59.

75. *Did She Or Didn't She?* by Mart Martin, page 37.

76. Salka Viertel was a Polish actress who had moved to America and lived with her three sons in a beach house in Santa Monica. The husband travelled and was absent. She was a successful screenwriter and Garbo's confidante and professional advisor.

77. *The Sewing Circle* by Axel Madsen, page 23.

78. *The Sewing Circle* by Axel Madsen, page 80.

79. *Laurence Olivier A Biography* by David Spoto, page 228.

80. *The Hidden (Queer and Jewish) Career of Danny Kaye* - interview with Michael Bronski, 7 April 2000. http://www.stephenbrophy.org/essay/dannykaye.html
81. *The Sewing Circle* by Axel Madsen, page 16.
82. *The Secret Sex Lives Of Famous People* by Irving, Amy, Sylvia Wallace & David Wallechinsky, page 110.
83. *The Secret Sex Lives Of Famous People* by Irving, Amy, Sylvia Wallace & David Wallechinsky, page 112.

Websites

http://www.bisexual.org
http://www.BiPlanet.com
www.angiebowie.com

The Essential Library

Conspiracy Theories by Robin Ramsay, £3.99

Do you think the X-Files is fiction? That Elvis is dead? That the US actually went to the moon? And don't know that the ruling elite did a deal with the extra-terrestrials after the Roswell crash in 1947... At one time, you could blame the world's troubles on the Masons or the Illuminati, or the Jews, or One Worlders, or the Great Communist Conspiracy. Now we also have the alien-US elite conspiracy, or the alien shape-shifting reptile conspiracy to worry about - and there are books to prove it as well! This book tries to sort out the handful of wheat from the choking clouds of intellectual chaff. For among the nonsensical Conspiracy Theory rubbish currently proliferating on the Internet, there are important nuggets of real research about real conspiracies waiting to be mined.

Ancient Greece by Mike Paine, £3.99

Western civilization began with the Greeks. From the highpoint of the 5th century BC through the cultural triumphs of the Alexandrian era to their impact on the developing Roman empire, the Greeks shaped the philosophy, art, architecture and literature of the Mediterranean world. Mike Paine provides a concise and well-informed narrative of many centuries of Greek history. He highlights the careers of great political and military leaders like Pericles and Alexander the Great, and shows the importance of the great philosophers like Plato and Aristotle. Dramatists and demagogues, stoics and epicureans, aristocrats and helots take their places in the unfolding story of the Greek achievement.

Black Death by Sean Martin, £3.99

The Black Death is the name most commonly given to the pandemic of bubonic plague that ravaged the medieval world in the late 1340s. From Central Asia the plague swept through Europe, leaving millions of dead in its wake. Between a quarter and a third of Europe's population died. In England the population fell from nearly six million to just over three million. The Black Death was the greatest demographic disaster in European history.

The Essential Library

The Crusades by Mike Paine, £3.99

The first crusade was set in motion by Pope Urban II in 1095 and culminated in the capture of Jerusalem from the Muslims four years later. In 1291 the fall of Acre marked the loss of the last Christian enclave in the Holy Land. This Pocket Essential traces the chronology of the Crusades between these two dates and highlights the most important figures on all sides of the conflict.

Alchemy & Alchemists by Sean Martin, £3.99

Alchemy is often seen as an example of medieval gullibility and the alchemists as a collection of eccentrics and superstitious fools. Sean Martin shows that nothing could be further from the truth. It is important to see the search for the philosopher's stone and the attempts to turn base metal into gold as metaphors for the relation of man to nature and man to God as much as seriously held beliefs. Alchemists like Paracelsus and Albertus Magnus were amongst the greatest minds of their time. This book traces the history of alchemy from ancient times to the 20th century, highlighting the interest of modern thinkers like Jung in the subject.

American Civil War by Phil Davies, £3.99

The American Civil War, fought between North and South in the years 1861-1865, was the bloodiest and most traumatic war in American history. Rival visions of the future of the United States faced one another across the battlefields and families and friends were bitterly divided by the conflict. This book examines the deep-rooted causes of the war, so much more complicated than the simple issue of slavery.

American Indian Wars by Howard Hughes, £3.99

At the beginning of the 1840s the proud tribes of the North American Indians looked across the plains at the seemingly unstoppable expansion of the white man's West. During the decades of conflict that followed, as the new world pushed onward, the Indians saw their way of life disappear before their eyes. Over the next 40 years they clung to a dream of freedom and a continuation of their traditions, a dream that was repeatedly shattered by the whites.

The Essential Library: Currently Available

Film Directors:

Woody Allen (Revised)	Tim Burton	Ang Lee
Jane Campion*	John Carpenter	Steve Soderbergh
Jackie Chan	Joel & Ethan Coen	Clint Eastwood
David Cronenberg	Terry Gilliam*	Michael Mann
Alfred Hitchcock	Krzysztof Kieslowski*	Roman Polanski
Stanley Kubrick	Sergio Leone	Oliver Stone
David Lynch	Brian De Palma*	
Sam Peckinpah*	Ridley Scott	
Orson Welles	Billy Wilder	
Steven Spielberg	Mike Hodges	

Film Genres:

Blaxploitation Films	Bollywood	French New Wave
Horror Films	Spaghetti Westerns	Vietnam War Movies
Vampire Films*	Heroic Bloodshed*	
Slasher Movies	Film Noir	

Film Subjects:

Laurel & Hardy	Marx Brothers	Animation
Steve McQueen*	Marilyn Monroe	The Oscars®
Filming On A Microbudget	Bruce Lee	Film Music

TV:

Doctor Who

Literature:

Cyberpunk	Philip K Dick	The Beat Generation
Agatha Christie	Sherlock Holmes	Noir Fiction*
Terry Pratchett	Hitchhiker's Guide	Alan Moore
Stephen King		

Ideas:

Conspiracy Theories	Nietzsche	UFOs
Feminism	Freud & Psychoanalysis	Bisexuality

History:

Alchemy & Alchemists	The Crusades	The Black Death
Jack The Ripper	The Rise Of New Labour	Ancient Greece
American Civil War	American Indian Wars	

Miscellaneous:

The Madchester Scene	Stock Market Essentials	Beastie Boys
How To Succeed As A Sports Agent		

Available at all good bookstores or send a cheque (payable to 'Oldcastle Books') to: **Pocket Essentials (Dept BSX), 18 Coleswood Rd, Harpenden, Herts, AL5 1EQ, UK**. £3.99 each (£2.99 if marked with an *) . For each book add 50p postage & packing in the UK and £1 elsewhere.